Earth Science
Discovering the secrets of the earth

PLATE TECTONICS

Grolier Educational

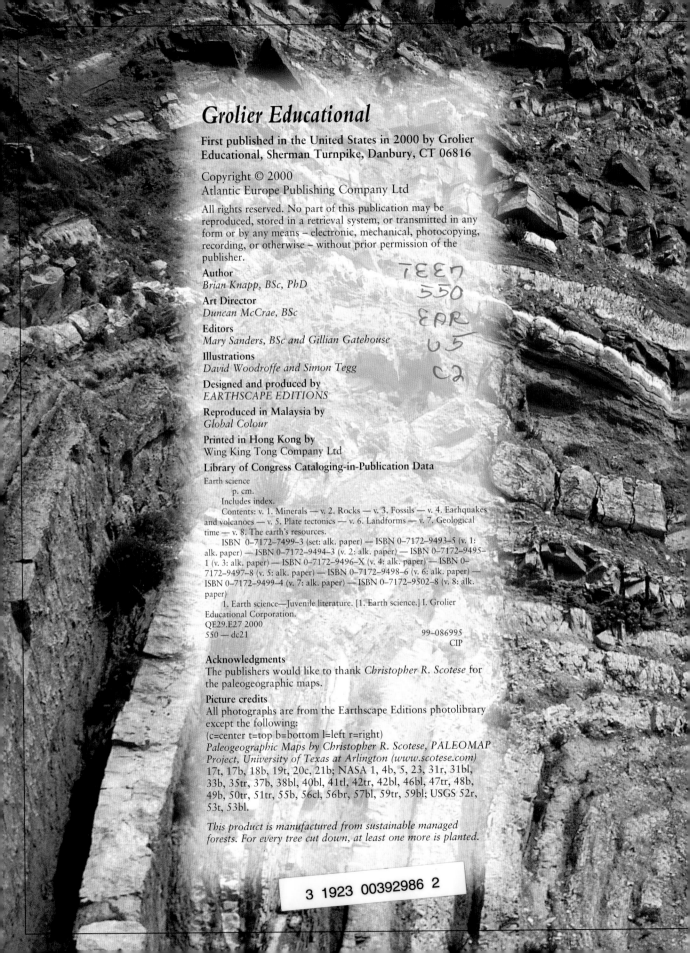

Grolier Educational

First published in the United States in 2000 by Grolier Educational, Sherman Turnpike, Danbury, CT 06816

Author
Brian Knapp, BSc, PhD

Art Director
Duncan McCrae, BSc

Editors
Mary Sanders, BSc and Gillian Gatehouse

Illustrations
David Woodroffe and Simon Tegg

Designed and produced by
EARTHSCAPE EDITIONS

Reproduced in Malaysia by
Global Colour

Printed in Hong Kong by
Wing King Tong Company Ltd

Library of Congress Cataloging-in-Publication Data

Earth science
        p. cm.
    Includes index.
        Contents: v. 1. Minerals — v. 2. Rocks — v. 3. Fossils — v. 4. Earhquakes and volcanoes — v. 5. Plate tectonics — v. 6. Landforms — v. 7. Geological time — v. 8. The earth's resources.
        ISBN 0–7172–7499–3 (set: alk. paper) — ISBN 0–7172–9493–5 (v. 1: alk. paper) — ISBN 0–7172–9494–3 (v. 2: alk. paper) — ISBN 0–7172–9495–1 (v. 3: alk. paper) — ISBN 0–7172–9496–X (v. 4: alk. paper) — ISBN 0–7172–9497–8 (v. 5: alk. paper) — ISBN 0–7172–9498–6 (v. 6: alk. paper) — ISBN 0–7172–9499–4 (v. 7: alk. paper) — ISBN 0–7172–9502–8 (v. 8: alk. paper)
        1. Earth science—Juvenile literature. [1. Earth science.] I. Grolier Educational Corporation.
QE29.E27 2000
550 — dc21   99–086995
                                                                        CIP

Acknowledgments
The publishers would like to thank *Christopher R. Scotese* for the paleogeographic maps.

Picture credits
All photographs are from the Earthscape Editions photolibrary except the following:
(c=center t=top b=bottom l=left r=right)
Paleogeographic Maps by Christopher R. Scotese, PALEOMAP Project, University of Texas at Arlington (www.scotese.com)
17t, 17b, 18b, 19t, 20c, 21b; NASA 1, 4b, 5, 23, 31r, 31bl, 33b, 35tr, 37b, 38bl, 40bl, 41tl, 42tr, 42bl, 46bl, 47tr, 48b, 49b, 50tr, 51tr, 55b, 56cl, 56br, 57bl, 59tr, 59bl; USGS 52r, 53t, 53bl.

This product is manufactured from sustainable managed forests. For every tree cut down, at least one more is planted.

Contents

Chapter 1:
The nature of plate tectonics

Have you ever wondered how the oceans and continents came to be the size and shape they are, or how coal was formed from tropical trees but is found in places that now have a cold climate? Have you ever wondered how mountains form or why there are volcanoes and earthquakes?

These are some of the many fundamental questions that many people have asked and that earth scientists have set out to answer.

Today it is believed that there is a single explanation for the way in which the world changes. It is called PLATE TECTONICS.

The word tectonics comes from the Greek *tekton*, meaning to move. The word plate comes from the idea that great slabs of the earth's crust are large and platelike, so the theory of plate tectonics is all about how large, platelike slabs of the earth's crust move around.

In recent years we have been able to see many of these large-scale features for the first time thanks to space photography. Many such pictures are used throughout this book.

(Right) This spectacular view from the Space Shuttle shows part of the Asian mountains that include the Himalayas and the Kun Lun Shan, the greatest land mountains in the world. Here you can see many ranges of snow-covered mountains that end abruptly in a high flat tableland, the Tibetan Plateau, that is covered in yellow sand. Plate tectonics sets out to explain how features like this came to be.

(Below) Special images from space allow us to see features of the earth that we never could before. This image shows the ocean floor. The long line of the Hawaiian Islands can be seen in the Pacific Ocean. Deep arc-shaped trenches (dark blue) can also be seen around much of the Pacific Ocean. A broad ridge can be seen running down the center of the Atlantic Ocean. More trenches outline an area around the Caribbean Sea. Such features provide vital clues that have helped scientists understand the nature of the great plates that make the surface of the earth.

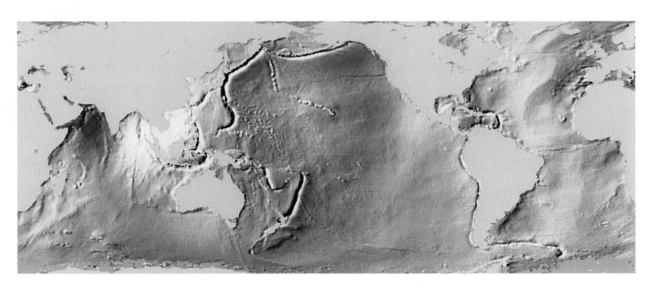

Inside the earth

Plate tectonics relies on an understanding of the internal workings of the earth. Only once we grasp how the layers of the earth behave can we explain many of the curious features of the surface.

The structure of the earth was discovered at the beginning of the 20th century by analyzing earthquake waves. It was found that there is a molten CORE at its center about half the diameter of the earth. It is made of extremely dense rock. Surrounding it is a shell of rock called the MANTLE, part of which can move very slowly when pressure is put on it. It is also very dense, but less dense than the core. The CRUST, the solid surface rocks on which we live, is a thin shell of brittle rock covering these massive inner layers, even thinner in proportion than the shell of an egg. The crust is the least dense of the layers that make up the earth.

(Below) The main layers of the earth. The diagram is not to scale.

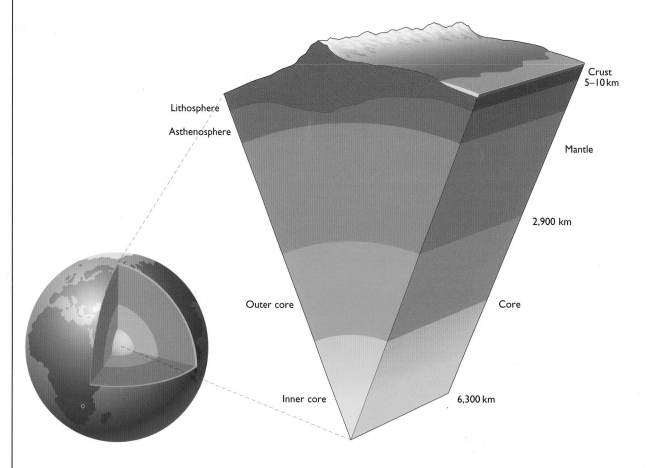

Lithosphere

Asthenosphere

Crust 5–10 km

Mantle

2,900 km

Outer core

Core

Inner core

6,300 km

The earth's heat comes primarily from the core. Layers of the earth close to the core are very hot, while those nearer the surface are cooler. The crust (which is cold) and the upper mantle (which is warm) are similar in the sense that their rocks are quite hard and brittle. They are often grouped together and called the LITHOSPHERE (from the Greek word *lithos*, meaning stone). The lithosphere is not very thick under the oceans, but it is very thick under the continents and particularly thick under mountains.

The floating crust

The lithosphere may be relatively thin, but it is still enormously heavy and exerts great pressure on the mantle below. Because the lower part of the mantle is able to change shape and move very slowly, this pressure allows the lithosphere to partly sink into the mantle, just as an iceberg partly sinks into the ocean water it floats on.

(*Below*) Earthquakes produce several types of waves that travel through the ground and make the earth ring like a bell.

Some waves (called P waves) can travel through solids and liquids; others (called S waves) can only travel through solids. When scientists discovered that there were no S waves recorded on the side of the earth opposite an earthquake, they were able to conclude that the core of the earth must be liquid—molten rock. They also found that there was a part of the earth that experienced no waves at all (called a shadow zone). Because the P waves were not present, scientists knew that they must be deflected in some way. This gave yet more clues to the structure of the earth and made it possible to work out the composition of many layers of the earth. (For a fuller explanation of earthquake waves see the book *Earthquakes and Volcanoes* in the *Earth Science* set.)

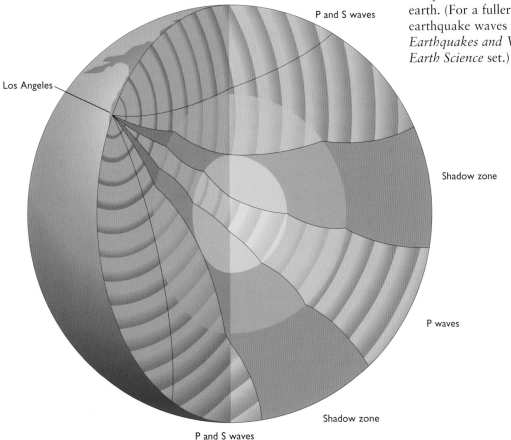

P and S waves

Los Angeles

Shadow zone

P waves

Shadow zone

P and S waves

When blocks float, the same <u>proportion</u> of a block is always above the liquid no matter what its size (just as 1/10th of an iceberg is always exposed, with 9/10ths below the water, no matter what the size of the iceberg). The thicker the block, the deeper it floats, but at the same time, the more of it rises above the surface. Mountains are therefore tall because they are places where the crust is thick and floats high in the mantle.

This explains why the lithosphere is deepest where the mountains exist. Every tall mountain must also have a deep "mountain root" to make it buoyant. The higher the land is, the deeper the mountain roots go. Roots are therefore thickest below mountain ranges and thinnest below the oceans.

The weak layer of the mantle called the **ASTHENOSPHERE** (from the Greek word *asthenes*, meaning "weak") moves under the weight of the lithosphere.

(Left and below) The lithosphere floats on the weak asthenosphere below, with the highest land also having the deepest roots.

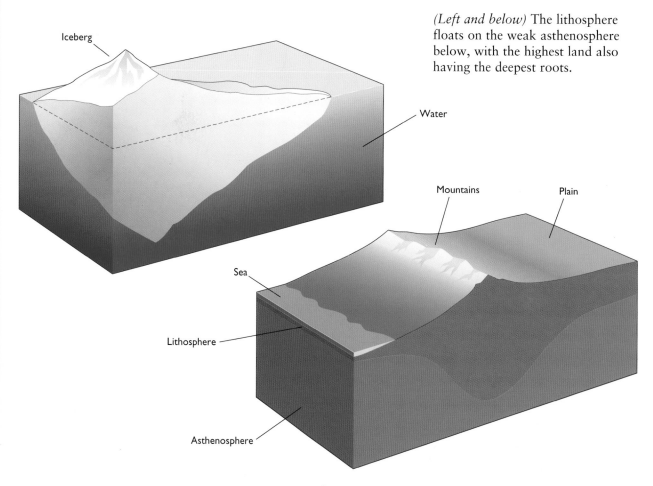

Because the lithosphere is very thin under the oceans—often no more than 6–7 kilometers—it does not float high in the asthenosphere, and that is why most of it is covered by water. The continents are much thicker—usually 30–40 kilometers thick and—at mountains—sometimes over 100 kilometers thick. As a result they float higher on the asthenosphere and are mainly dry land.

The moving mantle

If the asthenosphere is weak enough to allow the lithosphere to float on it, then it is also weak enough to flow as well. Here, then is the region in which movement can take place. Heat from the core makes the material in the asthenosphere behave like a slow-moving liquid, able to churn like water heated in a pan. Although the asthenosphere churns incredibly slowly (moving at only a few centimeters a year), it can, nonetheless, carry continents with it. Over hundreds of millions of years even slow speeds mount up to journeys of thousands of kilometers. That is how plate tectonics works.

The nature of plates

You can think of the lithosphere as something like a cracked eggshell. That is, the surface, which is very thin compared to the size of the earth, is mostly made of brittle rock that is cracked. There are about a dozen large fragments and some smaller ones. They are the TECTONIC PLATES. All have been given names.

The edges of the plates are not the same as the edges of the continents. Some edges are deep under the oceans. Plates therefore contain rocks that make both land and ocean floor.

But unlike a cracked eggshell, the plates do not stay still; instead, they slowly move across the earth's surface, driven by the churning forces in the mantle.

As the plates move around, they make oceans grow and shrink. When they collide, they form land bridges that allow living things to move from one plate to another and also create mountains that have enormous effects on the way the atmosphere moves and thus on the climates of the world.

Continents contain the world's oldest crustal rocks, yet the plates that contain the continents are not fixed in size or shape, nor do they last forever. When plates collide, their edges can be consumed entirely back into the mantle. This happens with ocean plates. It is happening along the edges of the Pacific Ocean Plate now (see page 36), and the whole of the small Juan de Fuca Plate is completely disappearing below the edge of the North American plate.

Conclusion

Plate tectonics helps explain how the earth has moved in a remarkable way. But the evidence for it has been hard to gather and has come from all kinds of sources. How people came to put the theory of plate tectonics together is the subject of the next chapter.

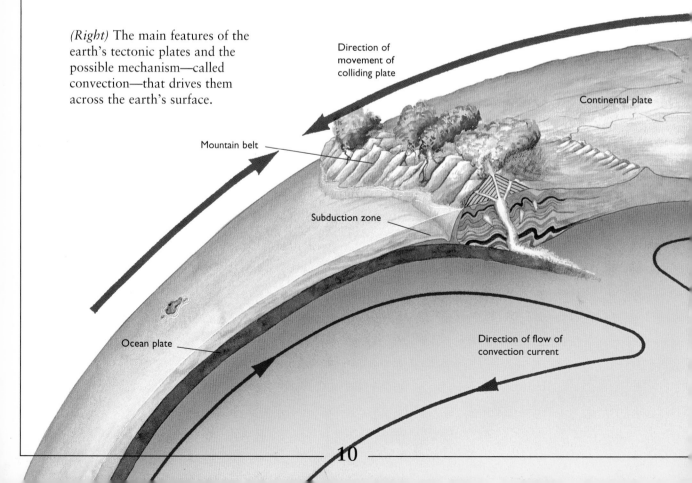

(Right) The main features of the earth's tectonic plates and the possible mechanism—called convection—that drives them across the earth's surface.

Direction of movement of colliding plate

Continental plate

Mountain belt

Subduction zone

Ocean plate

Direction of flow of convection current

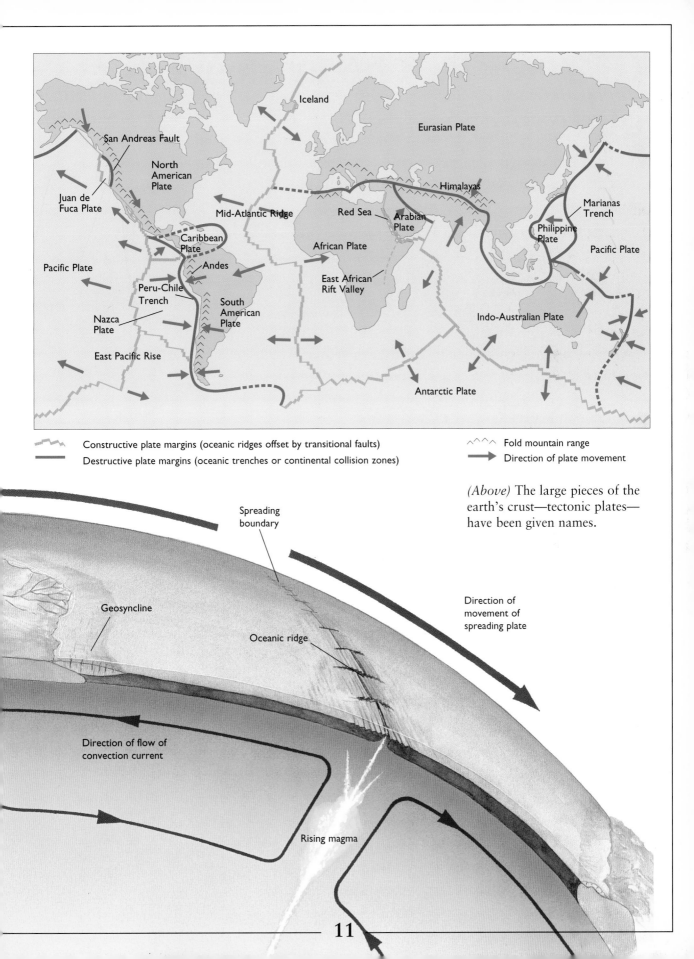

Iceland

Eurasian Plate

San Andreas Fault

North American Plate

Juan de Fuca Plate

Mid-Atlantic Ridge

Himalayas

Marianas Trench

Caribbean Plate

Red Sea

Arabian Plate

Philippine Plate

Pacific Plate

Pacific Plate

Andes

African Plate

Peru-Chile Trench

East African Rift Valley

Nazca Plate

South American Plate

Indo-Australian Plate

East Pacific Rise

Antarctic Plate

〰〰 Constructive plate margins (oceanic ridges offset by transitional faults)

〜〜 Destructive plate margins (oceanic trenches or continental collision zones)

ΛΛΛΛ Fold mountain range

➤ Direction of plate movement

(Above) The large pieces of the earth's crust—tectonic plates—have been given names.

Spreading boundary

Direction of movement of spreading plate

Geosyncline

Oceanic ridge

Direction of flow of convection current

Rising magma

Chapter 2: The evidence for plate tectonics

For many centuries people have known the size of the earth, but not what lay beneath its surface, nor how the mountains and continents had been formed. It was assumed that the earth was made of solid rock; but if this was so, then where did the material come from to make volcanoes? And if it was solid, then what caused earthquakes?

It was also assumed that the surface of the earth had been the same since the day of creation. But this was not supported by evidence, for it is clear that rivers continually erode material from the land and carry it out to the sea, thus changing the shape of both land and seabed.

(Below) There is evidence of rock called tillite in the southern continents dating back to Precambrian times. Its texture is just the same as the "boulder clay" or "glacial till" that is deposited by modern ice sheets. Hutton's principle of "The present is the key to the past" allows us to imagine that, for example, a billion years ago, glaciated landscapes looked much as they do today.

(Left) Fossil brachiopods still remain as rust-colored shells in this rock. They must have lived on a muddy estuary much as they might today. The muddy rock they are found in is over 400 million years old.

There were other problems, too. As people looked more carefully at the rocks, they found the fossilized remains of creatures that had once lived in the sea. For many years people assumed that they must have been the result of some recent catastrophic flood.

Because people believed that the earth was solid, it was difficult to understand how mountains had formed. It was widely believed that the earth was once much hotter than today and that it was now cooling. One theory suggested that as the earth cooled, it began to shrink. From time to time gravity then caused the solid crust to collapse down onto the shrinking core, wrinkling it to fit the ever-decreasing size of the core. The movement of the crust shrinking back on the core created the earthquakes, and volcanoes were excess material spurting through to the surface.

(Above) Dramatic cliffs such as this at Big Bend, Texas, show layer on layer of rocks of different kinds. They could surely not all have formed at the same time.

The present is the key to the past

It was the result of careful observation by a handful of scientists that eventually produced a new way of thinking about the earth. One of the earliest and most important people was James Hutton, a Scottish geologist whose study of rocks led him to believe that rocks in the past were formed in much the same way as rocks are being formed today. He concluded that "The present is the key to the past."

Hutton believed that the shape of the earth's surface did not need to be explained through catastrophic floods; it simply needed enormous amounts of time for quite commonplace processes to achieve everything around us.

Similarly shaped coasts

Many different strands of knowledge have added to the theory of plate tectonics. One of them was the idea of the present being the key to the past, as outlined above. Another powerful strand was produced by navigators, who sent back information that allowed map makers to build pictures of the world. Even though these maps were not completely accurate, people were struck by how much the coasts of South America and Africa looked like each other. They appeared to fit together as though they were parts of some global jigsaw puzzle. However, the coasts were 7,000 kilometers apart, so there was an intriguing puzzle that no one could solve.

As early as 1596 the Dutch map maker Abraham Ortelius suggested that the Americas were "torn away from Europe and Africa." He concluded, "The vestiges of the rupture reveal themselves, if someone brings forward a map of the world and considers carefully the coasts of the three [then known] continents."

Italian Antonio Snider-Pellegrini noticed that the earth had more ocean on one side than the other and so proposed that the continents were moving to correct the "lopsidedness" of the earth.

(Below) The apparent jigsaw fit of the Americas with Europe and Africa led people like Antonio Snider-Pellegrini to construct maps of what the world might once have looked like. However, they had no evidence for the reconstructions they proposed.

In 1666 François Paget in France tried to explain the vastness of the oceans in a different way. He thought it was as a result of the sinking of the part of the continent that used to join Africa and South America before Noah's flood.

An ancient supercontinent

Much of the speculation on the earth's continents and its mountains occurred during a period when more and more observations were being made.

One of the most remarkable discoveries in the 19th century was the result of geologists' collecting fossils from rocks all over the world. As they classified and grouped their fossils, they discovered some very remarkable things. Especially curious was that the same ancient species of land-dwelling creatures are found in the rocks of continents that are

(Below) The simplest way that the distribution of land-based and climate-dependent fossils can be explained is if the continents had once been joined and had also been in different places on the surface of the earth.

From this idea it is possible to reconstruct the historic position of the continents by matching up the distribution of similar fossils and rock structures such as fold mountains. Doing this allowed Wegener to develop the idea of a supercontinent called Pangaea.

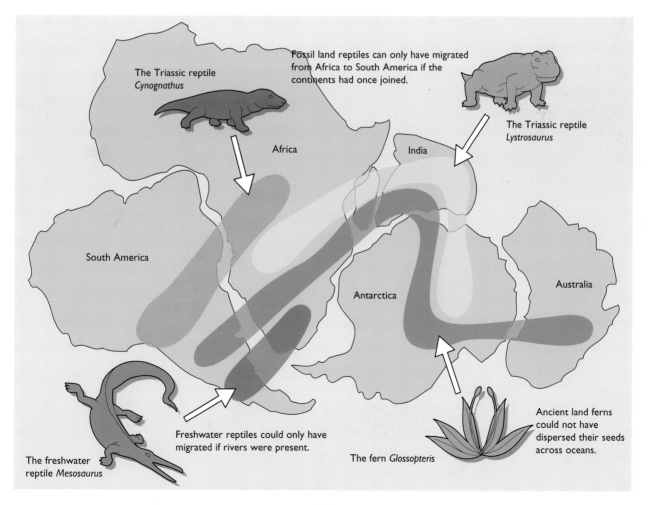

The Triassic reptile *Cynognathus*

Fossil land reptiles can only have migrated from Africa to South America if the continents had once joined.

The Triassic reptile *Lystrosaurus*

Africa

India

South America

Antarctica

Australia

Freshwater reptiles could only have migrated if rivers were present.

The freshwater reptile *Mesosaurus*

The fern *Glossopteris*

Ancient land ferns could not have dispersed their seeds across oceans.

now separated by thousands of kilometers. Because these species were all land-dwellers, they could not have swum across any ocean.

In trying to explain this observation, some people suggested that there must once have been a large ancient continent that had somehow broken into several fragments. Toward the end of the 19th century Austrian geologist Eduard Suess suggested that, for example, there once was an enormous southern continent, which he called Gondwana. Then parts of it sank, leaving the continents as we see them today.

The theory of continental drift

Some fossil evidence created problems that could not easily be solved by assuming that parts of the continents had sunk in their original positions. Many rocks, for example, are formed only under very special climatic conditions. Coal is made of the remains of tropical rainforest plants. Yet the distribution of coal deposits in the world today shows no relationship at all to the tropics. Coalfields are even found north of the Arctic Circle, which today is too cold for any kind of tree to grow.

The same problem was produced by looking at the pattern of many ancient sandstones. The grains that they contained showed them to have been formed in deserts. The world's greatest deserts all occur close to the tropics of Cancer and Capricorn. Yet the distribution of these ancient desert sandstones does not show any relationship to the present tropics.

Just as difficult to explain was the pattern of ancient ice sheets, some of whose rocks (called tillites) are now found close to the equator, where ice sheets could never have existed.

In 1908 American Frank Taylor returned to the idea that continents might move across the earth's surface and not just sink into the oceans. He suggested that the plowing of the continents across the earth's surface was the origin of mountain ranges, since the continents buckled up the seabed as they moved.

(Opposite, top) If the rocks that tell of an ancient glaciation are drawn on a map of the present day arrangement of continents, they make no sense when compared with the distribution of ice sheets in the last Ice Age. *(Opposite, bottom)* However, using the idea "the present is the key to the past," the continents can be moved around until the climate-related rocks are placed in correct positions with respect to the poles and equator. This is how the evidence of former climates was used to reconstruct continents by people such as Wegener. Climate-dependent rocks include coal (from swamps that only flourish in the tropics), glaciation (polar), and deserts (mainly subtropical).

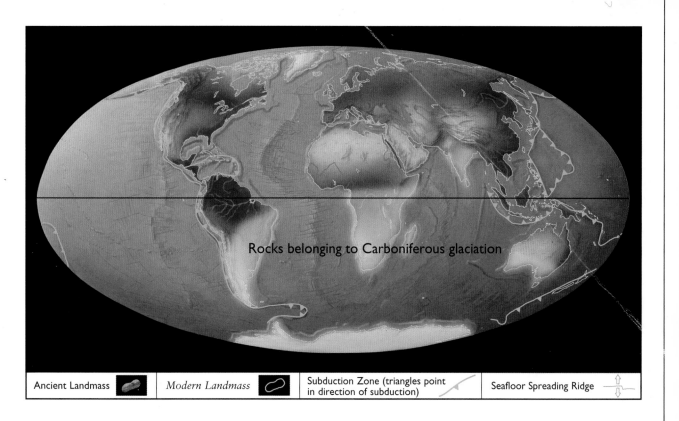

Rocks belonging to Carboniferous glaciation

Ancient Landmass		Modern Landmass		Subduction Zone (triangles point in direction of subduction)	Seafloor Spreading Ridge

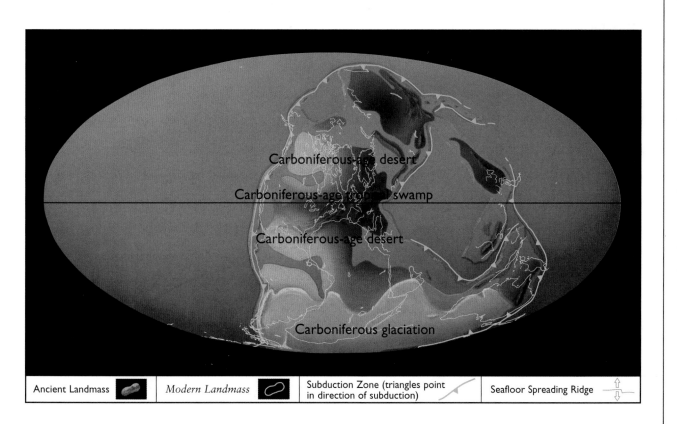

Carboniferous-age desert

Carboniferous-age tropical swamp

Carboniferous-age desert

Carboniferous glaciation

Ancient Landmass		Modern Landmass		Subduction Zone (triangles point in direction of subduction)	Seafloor Spreading Ridge

In Germany Alfred Wegener was studying ancient climates. In 1912, in an effort to make sense of the strange distribution of fossils, he, too, came to believe that the continents as we see them today are not in the same positions as they were in the past. He used patterns of similarly aged rocks and fossils to work out where the continents might have once been.

His conclusions were startling. He found that all of the continents had been joined together in a supercontinent (which he called Pangaea—meaning "all lands" in Greek) sometime around 300 million years ago (at the end of the Paleozoic ERA).

He suggested that the continents must somehow have drifted over the surface of the earth to reach the positions that we see them in today (maps with a modern interpretation of these changes are shown on this page and pages 19, 20, and 21). This is the theory called CONTINENTAL DRIFT, and Wegener's reconstruction was a major step toward developing the more complete theory of Plate Tectonics.

Using Wegener's conclusions as a foundation, Alexander Du Toit suggested that about 225 million

(Below) The map below, and those on pages 19, 20, and 21, show a modern interpretation of the movement of continents since the formation of Pangaea. These reconstructions are based on many pieces of evidence. Present-day continental outlines are shown for reference.

The map below shows the continents as they were in Permian times about 255 million years ago.

For a fuller description of the effects of the movements of the continents on rocks, landscape, and life see the book *Geological Time* in the *Earth Science* set.

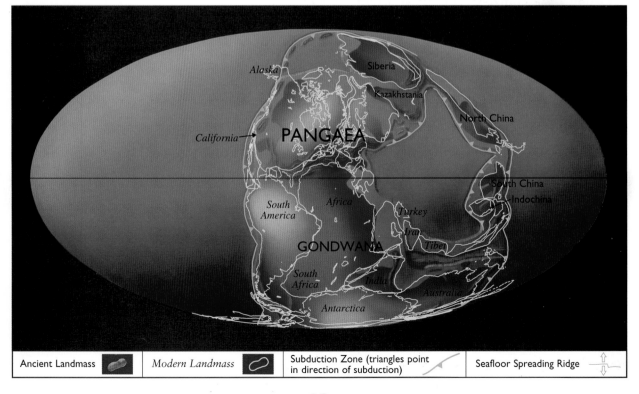

Ancient Landmass		*Modern Landmass*		Subduction Zone (triangles point in direction of subduction)	Seafloor Spreading Ridge	

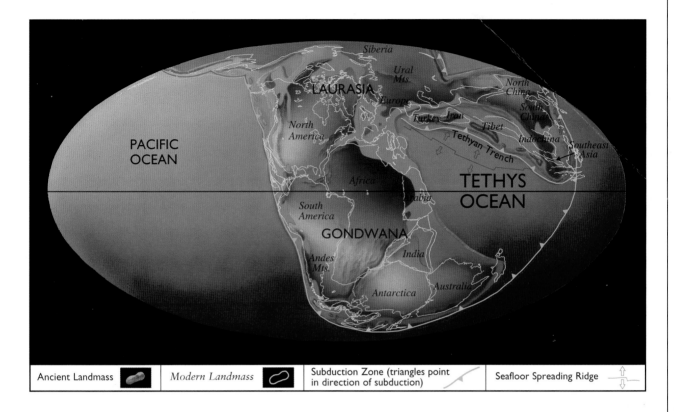

Labels on image: Siberia, Ural Mts., LAURASIA, North China, South China, Europe, North America, Turkey, Iran, Tibet, Indochina, Tethyan Trench, Southeast Asia, PACIFIC OCEAN, Africa, Arabia, TETHYS OCEAN, South America, GONDWANA, Andes Mts., India, Antarctica, Australia

| Ancient Landmass | Modern Landmass | Subduction Zone (triangles point in direction of subduction) | Seafloor Spreading Ridge |

years ago, Pangaea broke up into two large pieces. The northern one of these pieces he called Laurasia (comprising North America, Europe, and most of Asia) and the southern one (comprizing Antarctica, South America, Africa, Oceania, and India) he called Gondwana. He then suggested that these two continents further broke up into smaller pieces to make most of the continents we see today. The breakup of the continents caused ancient oceans to close and new ones to open.

Like Taylor and others before him, Wegener and Du Toit had the problem of suggesting a believable mechanism that would move the vastness of the earth's crust slowly through the ages. At the time, however, because most people thought that the earth was solid, few believed that continents could move, and this theory was dismissed.

In 1929 Arthur Holmes in England used new information about the structure of the earth to propose a mechanism that would drive continental drift. He pointed out (as we have already described

(Above) The continents as they may have looked in Jurassic times about 190 million years ago.

in Chapter 1) that the crust was very thin compared with the mantle below, and that any movement in the mantle would almost certainly drag the crust with it. He therefore suggested that slow, steady convection, or churning, in the mantle could be the cause. But again, this idea seemed, at the time, too fantastic to believe, and Holmes could find no direct evidence to back up his suggestion.

(Below) The continents as they may have looked in Cretaceous times about 94 million years ago.

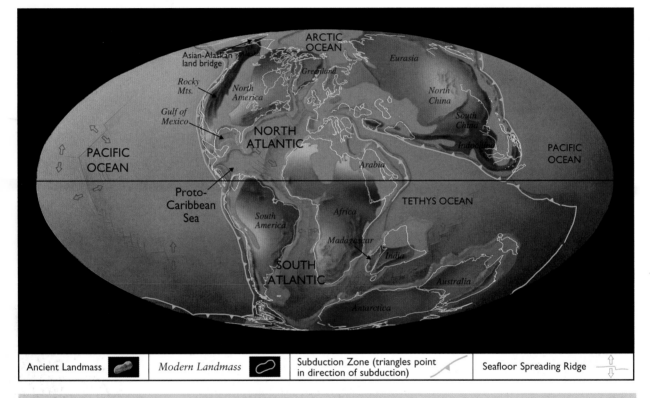

Ancient Landmass	Modern Landmass	Subduction Zone (triangles point in direction of subduction)	Seafloor Spreading Ridge

The principle of convection

Convection is a process that happens in liquids heated from below. The hot liquid expands and becomes less dense than the liquid above. As a result, it begins to rise. As the hot, less dense material rises, cooler, more dense material sinks down to take its place. In this way material constantly churns as long as heating from below continues.

Although at the beginning of the 20th century, when Alfred Wegener proposed the idea that continents drift, his ideas were dismissed because people thought that the earth was entirely solid, there is little doubt that the tectonic plates do actually move, although very slowly. The problem of what causes the movement remains.

It is likely that the upper mantle can flow very slowly, even if it is not actually molten. The way the mantle behaves may be similar to the way that red-hot steel moves. Under pressure the solid actually changes shape as crystals within it melt when they are stressed and re-form when the stress is removed.

Some pockets in the upper mantle do contain molten materials, and they are the sources of the plumes that make their way to the surface and form the world's volcanoes.

The concept of convection has very important consequences, for, if true, it tells us that there must be places where lighter rock rises (for example, plumes of magma that make volcanoes) and where denser rock sinks (for example, at ocean trenches).

The reason that it was so hard to find conclusive evidence for drift was that the evidence was not on land but under the oceans, and at the time, scientists had no means of discovering what lay below the ocean surface. In the 1960s new evidence was found by examining the pattern of fossil magnetism locked away in rocks on the world's ocean floors.

Paleomagnetism

One of the most important steps in proving that the earth's crust really could move came with the invention of new technology. It was already known that rocks could be magnetized—lodestone (an ironstone in which strong magnetism naturally occurs) had been known for thousands of years. It was also known that as molten rocks cooled, they locked inside them a record of the earth's magnetic field. Some rocks are therefore natural fossil compasses, holding a record of the magnetism of the past.

Magnetism depends only on the position of the earth's magnetic pole. When ancient rocks were examined for their fossil magnetism, a curious result

(Below) The continents as they may have looked in Miocene times about 14 million years ago.

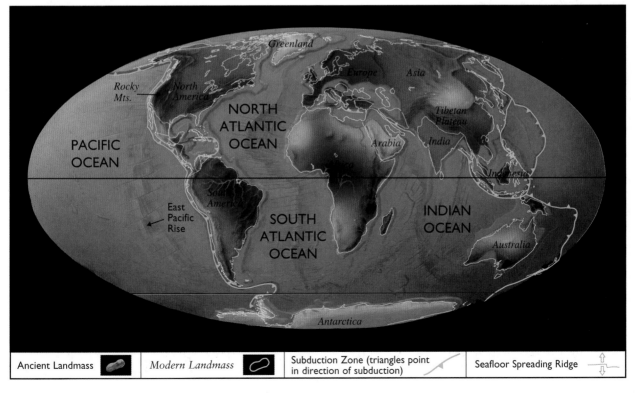

| Ancient Landmass | | Modern Landmass | | Subduction Zone (triangles point in direction of subduction) | Seafloor Spreading Ridge |

emerged. The fossil magnets did not always point to the present north pole. If you had been able to stand where Europe is today in Precambrian times, for example, your compass would have pointed toward Hawaii as the North Pole.

In fact, fossil magnets in rocks of different ages point to different places on the earth's surface. Even rocks of the same age but from different continents also point to different places on the earth's surface!

It is, of course, impossible for the earth to have several magnetic poles in different places at the same time. Thus scientists were led to the conclusion that the continents must have been in different places in the past. This is how fossil magnetism came to be used to reconstruct the positions of the continents in the past.

Using fossil magnetism, it became possible to reconstruct the geography of the earth in the past, not just during the period when the continents were all together.

When the positions of the continents were reconstructed using fossil magnetism, they showed that rocks older than 300 million years all shared a common magnetic pole. Here then, was independent evidence that Pangaea had once existed. The case for continental drift had been made.

The ocean floor

Although the positions of the ancient continents had become clear using fossil magnetism and the fossil record, almost nothing was known about the crust below the oceans until quite recently.

The development of echo-sounding equipment and then sonar changed all this. Using these techniques, it soon became clear that the oceans had ranges of tall, broad mountains running down their centers and that the ranges joined, curving across the earth like the sewn seam on a baseball. Together they made the longest mountain range in the world.

(Below) These reconstructions show how the locked-in magnetism of rocks can help find the ancient positions of the continents. It works on the principle that the earth only has one pair of magnetic poles.

In the upper diagram (which shows the continents in their modern positions) the direction of the locked-in magnetism is shown for rocks of the same age on three continents. The magnetism points to three different poles.

The lower diagram shows that it is, however, possible to rearrange the continents around a common pole. This suggests how they were arranged at the time the magnetism was locked into the rocks. In this case it can be seen that all three continents used to fit together (to make the ancient supercontinent called Pangaea).

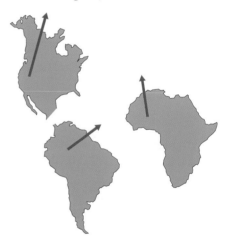

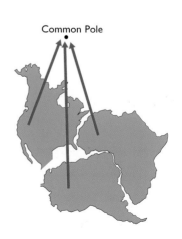

Common Pole

(Above) Tenerife, the largest island in the Canary Island archipelago. Pico de Teide, its volcanic peak, reaches 3,718 meters above the sea, making it the highest point in the Atlantic Ocean. The summit CALDERA (which is about 16 kilometers across at its widest) contains active volcanoes. Nobody could explain the presence of such volcanic islands in the ocean before the concept of plate tectonics was formulated.

The range runs for some 60,000 kilometers and completely encircles the earth. It is hundreds of kilometers and sometimes more than a thousand kilometers broad.

Surveys also showed that much of the midocean mountain chain has a deep trench, or RIFT VALLEY, along its crest. A rift valley only occurs where the crust is stretching, making rocks crack apart. When this happens, some blocks sink.

Further investigations showed that the ocean mountain chains were often matched by deep, narrow TRENCHES near their margins. They were the deepest places in the world, reaching down in some places more than 11 kilometers. Most trenches were curved, or arc-shaped in plan, and occurred just offshore or beyond strings of islands. These islands, too, followed a curved plan, which is how they came to be called ISLAND ARCS.

(Left and below) If the oceans were very old and unchanging, the ocean floors should be level and covered in layer after layer of sediment, the oldest at the bottom and the youngest everywhere at the surface, as shown in the top diagram. However, samples of the rocks obtained by the research ship *Glomar Challenger* in 1968 showed very little sediment on the ocean floor. The youngest rock was near the middle, and rocks were older toward the edges of the oceans, as shown in the bottom diagram.

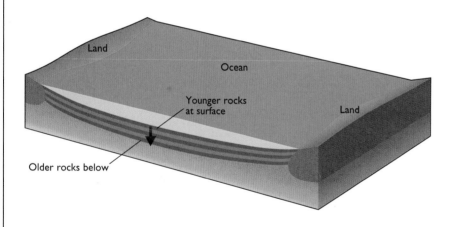

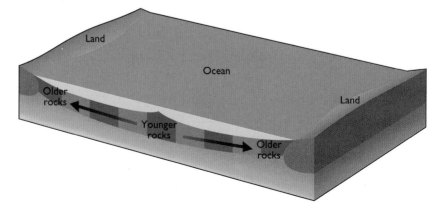

The most spectacular part of the ocean mountain system proved to be the Mid-Atlantic Ridge. The Pacific Ocean, by contrast, contains the most island arcs and the world's deepest trenches. This contrast between the world's greatest oceans proved very puzzling, for it suggested that different things were occurring in each ocean.

But this was not the only puzzle, for the broad expanses of ocean floor that separates the midoceanic ridges from the continents is crisscrossed by a huge network of cliffs and basins. This pattern suggested that the ocean floor was split up into blocks moving independently of one another.

Seafloor spreading

Scientists had believed that the oceans and continents were much the same age and had existed for almost as long as the earth—at least 4 billion years. Therefore the sediment layer on the ocean floor should everywhere have been very thick. In 1947 seismologists on the U.S. research ship *Atlantis* found that the sediment layer on the floor of the Atlantic was much thinner than had been supposed. The only answer could be that the ocean floors were not old, but new and able to renew themselves in some way.

Magnetic stripes

At the same time as echo sounders were being used to find out the shape of the ocean floor, other ships were trailing magnetometers, instruments that measure the magnetism of the rocks below.

Basalt is an iron-rich, volcanic rock that contains a strongly magnetic mineral (magnetite). Grains of magnetite behave like little magnets and align themselves with the orientation of the earth's magnetic field. When magma cools to form solid volcanic rock, the alignment of the magnetite grains is "locked in" and so records the direction

(Below) When scientists studied the magnetism in ocean-floor basalt rocks, they discovered a pattern of bands of low and high magnetism.

Places where the magnetism is high show where the earth's magnetic field is reinforced by the fossil magnetism of the rocks. Places where the magnetism is low show where the earth's magnetic field is being reduced by the effect of the fossil magnetism locked in the ocean-floor rocks.

When these bands were mapped, it was found that there was a mirror image of magnetic bands on either side of a midocean ridge. This could only have come about if the ocean floor was spreading apart. The colors used on this diagram show the effect of bands of magnetism on the ocean floor. It is the same pattern as obtained by measuring the age of the rocks.

of the earth's magnetic field at the time of cooling. Basalt is therefore one of the best rocks for preserving a record of the earth's magnetic field. Although basalt is not especially common on land, it covers almost the whole of the world's ocean floors.

The first map of the magnetic survey was made of the eastern Pacific Ocean. The scientists who made the measurements had expected to find a complicated and confused pattern of the kind seen on land. Instead, they found a simple pattern of bands with higher magnetism separated by bands of lower magnetism. On a map they look like simple stripes.

It was soon obvious that the magnetic bands on one side of the East Pacific Rise were a mirror image of those on the other side. This pattern seemed possible only if the seafloor was spreading out from midocean ridges.

So, quite quickly the evidence was building up to show that the ocean floors were spreading outward from their central ridges.

(Below) This map shows the patterns of magnetic stripes that have been found in the world's oceans. All show evidence of seafloor spreading.

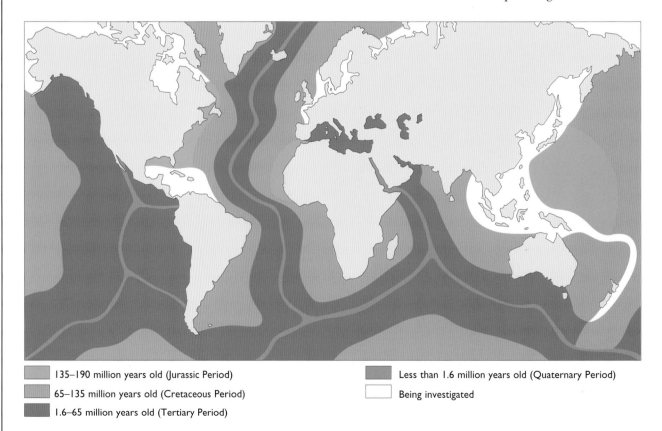

	135–190 million years old (Jurassic Period)
	65–135 million years old (Cretaceous Period)
	1.6–65 million years old (Tertiary Period)
	Less than 1.6 million years old (Quaternary Period)
	Being investigated

Plate tectonics

Clearly, all of these spectacular findings must be part of a single global process. Harry Hess in the United States was one of the first to find a way to bring all of the pieces of evidence together in a meaningful way.

He began by using Holmes's idea of mantle convection currents. He suggested that the midocean ridges were places where the convection currents rose to the surface. Trenches were places where convection currents dived down, and ocean-floor plains, crisscrossed by their great FAULTS, were places where the ocean floor was moving across the surface of the earth in great slabs.

Hess then went on to add detail to this overall picture. He suggested that when the rising convection brought magma to the surface, it welled out of fissures and then cooled to form new ocean crust. Over hundreds of millions of years this newly formed crust would be slowly transferred across the ocean floor and eventually consumed in the ocean trenches. In this way he was able to account for the ocean floor being youngest near the ridges and oldest near the continents and for the symmetrical pattern of rocks on both sides of the ocean ridges.

Thus, for the first time people realized that when they looked at Iceland, they were looking at a part of the Mid-Atlantic Ridge and that they were therefore able to study the ocean floor. And what they found was fresh lava coming from fissures. Not only that, but by dating the rocks of Iceland, it was clear that the rocks were formed in bands, with the oldest at the eastern and westernmost parts of the island, and the newest regions in the center, where the lava was still actively flowing. This, then, was clear evidence that the ocean floors were splitting apart and that the oceans were spreading outward from the midocean ridges. Plate tectonics had been put firmly into first place among earth science theories.

er 3: Plate boundaries

plates completely cover the earth's
any plate moves, it must affect all of its
ors. So, for example, if two plates pull apart in
place, they must collide with others on their far
es and also scrape along their neighbors to the side
of them. This is a complicated pattern, and so we will
first summarize all the types of boundaries, then look
in detail at each one.

Summary of plate boundaries

Plates that are pulling apart (spreading plates)
produce ocean floors, oceanic mountains, and
volcanoes; colliding plates produce earthquakes,
volcanoes, and above all, mountain belts; while
plates that scrape past one another produce
only earthquakes.

Below the crust the mantle is under enormous
pressure. As plates pull apart, some of the molten
mantle rock from the asthenosphere (called MAGMA)
is able to well up to the surface as lava and gas.
The spreading plate boundaries are rather like
a wound that will not heal. The plates pull

(Below) The types of plate
boundaries.

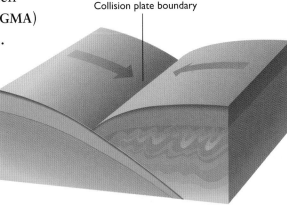

Collision plate boundary

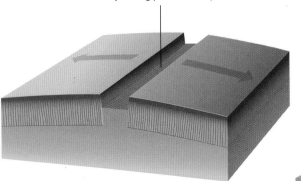

Spreading plate boundary

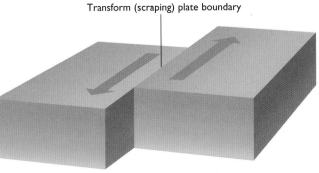

Transform (scraping) plate boundary

apart, and magma wells up and seals the crack for a while; but the plates soon open the crack again, causing more volcanic activity.

Where plates meet, enormous pressures build up, often forcing one plate under the other. As a result, one plate moves down into the earth, where it remelts into the mantle again. The places in which the plates are pushed down are called SUBDUCTION ZONES. They are marked in the oceans by long, narrow ocean trenches, the deepest places on earth, and also by patterns of volcanic mountains that are called island arcs.

The edges of some plates do not fold down into dramatic trenches, but slowly buckle downward, creating giant elongated sags in the crust known as GEOSYNCLINES that are natural collecting points (sinks) for sediment eroded from the land. In many cases the buckling more or less matches the rate at which sediment is laid down, so they do not make deep ocean trenches. Nevertheless, enormous thicknesses of sediment can form in geosynclines. When two plates eventually collide, these geosynclines are crushed into new MOUNTAIN BELTS.

Spreading plate boundaries

Spreading boundaries are places where the plates pull apart. Huge tensions form in the plates, and they must be marked by faults. Rift valleys form, both along the midoceanic ridges and also on land.

As magma rises, it swells and domes up the land, then splits it and pulls it apart. The molten rock then flows into the splits before cooling and becoming part of the new crust. As more splitting takes place, new material wells up, and the older material moves to one side. In this way the materials formed at a spreading boundary gradually move away from the active boundary as though they are on a conveyor belt.

Most of the spreading boundaries are deep under the oceans. They appear at the surface only in Iceland (described on page 27), the Middle East, and East Africa, described here.

East Africa and the Middle East show the spreading boundary at its earliest stages. The split is pivoting at a spot somewhere in northern Israel. The split is therefore narrowest in the Middle East, where it forms the Jordan Rift Valley and contains the Sea of Galilee. The split widens and divides to form the Gulf of Aqaba and the Gulf of Suez. It widens further to form the Red Sea, one of the world's great rift valleys. A branch of the split follows down through East Africa, creating the East African Rift Valley, and this, too, branches apart, to make two arms, each occupied by long finger lakes like Lake Malawi. A plateau remains between the branches, and it is, in part, filled by Lake Victoria.

Everywhere in this zone the underlying tension shows not only in the rift valley shapes but also in the way that magma is rising to the surface, creating a string of volcanoes, such as the giant volcanic mountains of Africa, Mount Kenya and Mount Kilimanjaro.

At the moment, the Red Sea is the world's newest ocean, but East Africa may split apart and create an even newer ocean. If this happens, the Horn of Africa will become a large island.

The splitting that we are witnessing in East Africa and the Middle East is the way that the Atlantic probably first developed when North America split away from Europe. The rocks of northwestern Scotland, Ireland, and northern England are shot through with SILLS and DIKES as evidence of this time, as are many of the rocks in Greenland and along the eastern seaboard of North America.

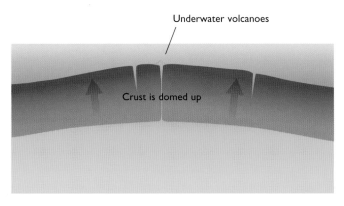

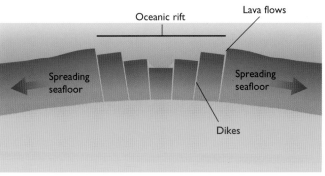

(Above) Spreading boundaries involve rift valleys and the upwelling of basalt as volcanoes.

(Below) The Middle East and East Africa lie on one of the world's most active spreading boundaries. The map shows the movement of Africa away from Asia. The red triangles are historically active volcanoes.

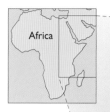

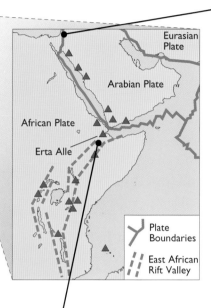

(Below) This view from space shows the Denakil Desert, Eritrea, and Ethiopia. The view looks northeast over the southern part of the Red Sea, an area of the Great Rift Valley called the Afar Triangle.

The active volcano, Erta Alle (dark gray area near the center of the photograph), is a large shield volcano. It has been in a constant state of eruption since the late 1960s. Across the Red Sea the Hijaz Mountains are visible.

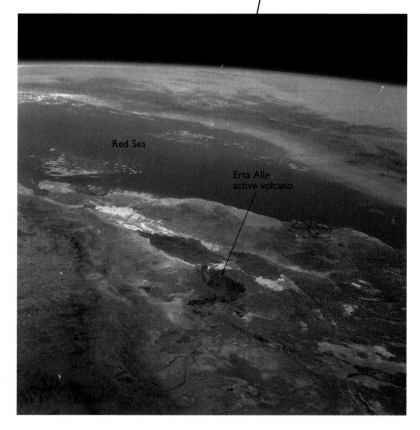

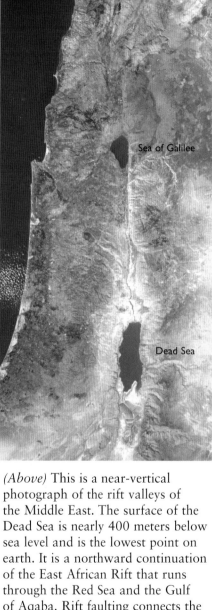

(Above) This is a near-vertical photograph of the rift valleys of the Middle East. The surface of the Dead Sea is nearly 400 meters below sea level and is the lowest point on earth. It is a northward continuation of the East African Rift that runs through the Red Sea and the Gulf of Aqaba. Rift faulting connects the Dead Sea with the Jordan River Valley and through the Sea of Galilee; however, northward in Lebanon the rifting splays out into a series of north-northeast trending faults. Rifting has yet to go this far.

Collision plate boundaries

Plates are pieces of the lithosphere that are in some places fringed with ocean crust and in other places fringed by continental crust. Ocean crust is thin and made of dense material. Continental crust is much thicker and also made of less dense material. When plates meet, the crusts have to shorten in some way. This may be by both plate edges crumpling, or by one plate riding over the other and forcing it down into the mantle.

When ocean crust meets ocean crust, two dense but thin pieces of crust collide. The one that is pushed down is usually the one moving most quickly. When ocean crust meets continental crust, the ocean crust is pushed down because it is thinner and denser.

Where continents collide, two thick plates of equal density meet, and neither is pushed into the mantle. Instead, they crush together and remain on the surface to form new mountain belts. In this way continents survive plate movements, while oceans do not. The continents grow slowly through time. This is why the cores of the continents are the oldest parts of the crust (see Chapter 4). Similarly, because it is always the ocean that is destroyed and renewed, the oceans are the newest parts of the crust.

When plates scrape past one another (transform plate boundaries), rather than collide, no crust is destroyed or created. Only earthquakes mark these boundaries.

Subduction zones

Subduction zones are long belts where ocean crust and continental crust collide. Here enormous pressure builds up until finally one of the plate edges is pushed down into the mantle and destroyed (subducted). In this way the creation of new material at spreading boundaries is matched by the destruction of older material at subduction zones.

Subduction zones are very complicated places, and many processes happen at the same time. Essentially, as one plate is pushed below the other, enormous amounts of friction have to be overcome. This happens in a series of small, rapid movements separated by long periods when the stress builds up again. Each time the stress is relieved, it creates an earthquake. Earthquakes form all along the surface of the subducting plate until the depth at which it melts.

The sinking plate is pushed under the surviving plate at a sharp angle, often 20–60 degrees. The sinking plate may not melt until it is more than 200 kilometers below the surface, so earthquakes can be generated throughout this zone. This means that the shallowest earthquakes occur close to the place where the plate sinks and are deeper (but no less violent) away from the line of collision.

The actual line of collision is often marked clearly on the earth's surface by long, very deep, and narrow trenches. The deepest of these trenches, the Mariana Trench, is over 11 kilometers deep.

The collision causes the surviving plate to crumple and thicken, in turn making the seabed shallower, even possibly rising above sea level. As the subducting plate sinks, its rocks get hotter and hotter and begin to melt.

(Below) Ocean-ocean and ocean-continent subduction zones are commonly marked by chains of active volcanoes. Ash can be seen pouring from one of the Kamchatka Peninsula's volcanoes at the northeastern tip of Asia.

Some of the molten material then rises in the form of plumes of molten magma, and many plumes find their way to the surface, where they erupt as volcanoes, creating chains of volcanic mountains.

Ocean-ocean collisions

Collisions can occur between two pieces of ocean plate. Both plates contain the same density rocks, and so it is usually the faster moving plate that subducts.

When this happens (as, for example, in the western and southern Pacific), the surviving plate thickens and forms long chains of islands, usually crescent- or arc-shaped. They are known as island arcs. The bowing part of the arc faces the direction of the collision, with the ocean trenches on their oceanward sides. The Marianas are examples of ocean-ocean collisions, as are the Japanese Islands, the Kuriles, the Aleutians, and the Philippines.

(Below) Ocean-ocean collisions produce island mountain ranges that are made entirely of ocean crustal material.

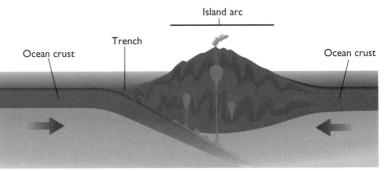

(Below) Plate movements produce numerous earthquakes. In this way the earthquake pattern can be used to identify the plate boundaries.

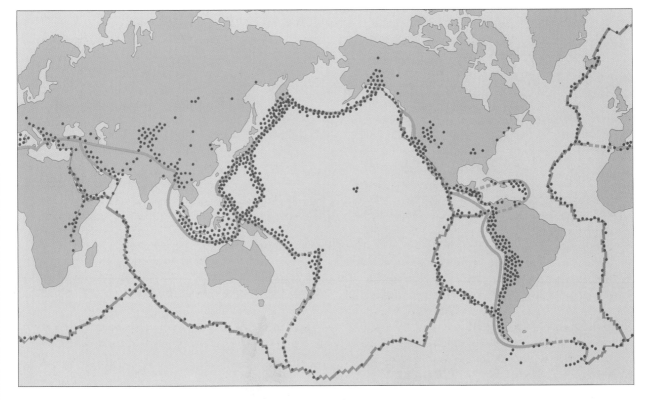

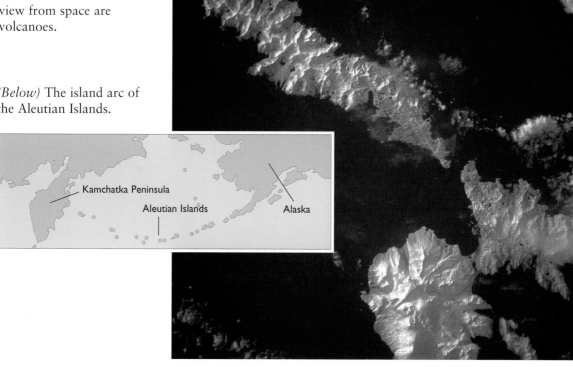

(Right) The Aleutian Islands are an island arc system in the northwest Pacific. All of the mountains seen in this view from space are volcanoes.

(Below) The island arc of the Aleutian Islands.

Kamchatka Peninsula

Aleutian Islands

Alaska

The island arcs of the Pacific

Starting from the Cascade Mountains in the northwest of the United States, it is possible to trace a chain of volcanic mountains north and west through Alaska, westward across into the Aleutian Islands, then down through the Kamchatka Peninsula to Japan. All of these volcanoes rise out of the sea, even those in mainland Alaska, rather than punching through a slab of continent. They all occur because here the Pacific Plate is being subducted beneath the surrounding plates, mainly small ocean plates lying off the main continents.

Taiwan is the only island that does not fit this pattern and is, in fact, part of the Asian continent. The Philippines are also complicated because they are being produced as a result of two subduction zones, one to the east of the islands and one to the west. The mountainous landscape of the Philippine Islands is a consequence both of subduction of the South China Sea floor eastward beneath Luzon and of subduction of the Philippine Sea floor westward

beneath the southern Philippine Islands. Both vulcanism and the crushing of the crust have formed the mountains here.

The island arcs continue across Indonesia through to the New Hebrides Islands.

The mountains of New Guinea consist of folded and faulted volcanic and sedimentary rocks. The volcanic rocks include both ancient seafloor and old island arcs that were thrust up and onto the northern edge of Australia.

The island arcs continue through the Tonga and Kermadec Islands to the North Island of New Zealand. The North island is mainly the result of volcanic activity, but the South Island is the result of the crust being squashed, rather than subducted. Thus the southern New Zealand Alps are not volcanic, but mainly SEDIMENTARY and METAMORPHIC rocks.

All of the island chains have the same type of landscape, consisting of steep volcanic cones in between which are regions of much lower lying land.

Ocean-continent collisions

Continental plates are not only much thicker than ocean plates, but also made of less dense rocks. When ocean plates collide with continental plates, therefore, the ocean plate always subducts, and at the same time, the sediments at the edge of the continent are often thrust back over the continent to form tall mountains.

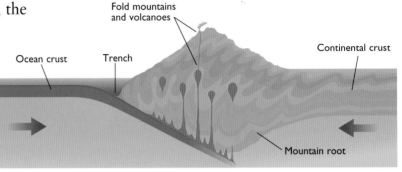

(Below) Ocean-continent collisions produce mountain ranges that combine folded sediment with volcanic material.

Ocean crust · Trench · Fold mountains and volcanoes · Continental crust · Mountain root

Many of the same features are found where oceans plates and continental plates collide as where ocean plates collide with each other. The line of collision is marked by a deep trench. One of the biggest of these trenches is called the Peru-Chile Trench, and it runs down most of the length of South America.

Here, the oceanic Nazca Plate is being subducted under the South American Plate, crushing the rocks at the edge of the South American Plate and pushing them over the top of a large part of the South American continent to create the foundations of the Andes Mountains. The crust is crushed, making it narrower, but also pushing all the rocks higher. At the same time, as the Nazca Plate descends, it releases magma that produces the volcanoes that make some of the towering summits of this spectacular mountain range. Again, earthquakes are also a feature of the rapid collision.

The crust that is crushed at these edges is under much less intense pressure than when major continents collide, as we will see later in this chapter. Thus, for example, the Andes have folded rocks that show much less metamorphism in them than is true for the Himalayas. These rocks are less resistant to erosion, and so the landscape is less rugged than where it is dominated by metamorphic rocks. In the Andes many of the most impressive glacial valleys

(Above) The South American cordillera.

and canyons have been cut simply because the rock is so much less resistant to erosion.

FOLDING and THRUST FAULTING are widespread. In the east the rocks tend to be folded, whereas in the west, where subduction had greater influence, the rocks are faulted and pushed over one another across great thrust planes. These variations are especially well shown in the widest part of the Andes system, for example, in Bolivia, where each of the mountain ranges is distinctively different in character.

(Below) The active volcanoes in the Andes are part of the world's most dramatic ocean-continent collision zone.

The snow-capped peaks in the middle-left of this picture taken from space are the high volcanoes of Ampato, Hualca Hualca, and Sabancaya that sit on the southern edge of the Canyon del Colca, Peru.

In northern South America, in the region of the Caribbean Sea, there are several small plates, and their movements have also created mountains. Here you can find many ocean-ocean and ocean-continent mountains in one small area.

The mountain range along the coast of Venezuela has many similarities to the Andes, for it was formed when the Caribbean Sea Plate was subducted southward beneath Venezuela. The Lesser Antilles, by contrast, are volcanic islands that form a typical island arc and show where a part of the floor of the North Atlantic Ocean pushes under the Caribbean Sea Plate.

Most of the other main islands in the northern Caribbean, such as Puerto Rico, Cuba, and Jamaica, are similar to Venezuela in origin.

(Above) Ocean-continent collisions produce a mixture of sedimentary and volcanic rocks.

The Nazca Plate is moving below the South American plate at about 100 millimeters per year. This has created a line of volcanoes, including South America's highest volcanic mountain, Ojos del Salado (6,893 meters). However, the highest mountain on the continent, Mount Aconcagua (6,959 meters), is made of folded and faulted sediments and contains no volcanic material at all.

(Left) Seen from space, the Andes Mountains rise like a wall from the Pacific Ocean. They mark the line of the ocean-continent collision zone. The rocks are not, however, all volcanoes; volcanoes simply rise through thick, folded beds of sedimentary rock.

The North American Cordillera

The word CORDILLERA is used for any mountain belt that contains mountains of various ages. The North American Cordillera extends from Alaska down the whole western side of North America to Mexico.

At the moment, subduction is occurring in two small places. One is where the small Juan de Fuca Plate is disappearing beneath northern California, Oregon, Washington, and southern British Columbia. It is an ocean-continent collision that is producing the Cascade chain of volcanoes, including recently active Mount Saint Helens. At the same time, the much larger Pacific Plate is moving north-northwest, almost parallel to the west coast of North America, and only causing subduction under the Alaskan archipelago, where it has built the volcanic chain that forms the Aleutian Islands and the Alaskan Peninsula.

Most of the North American Cordillera was formed between about 170 million and 40 million years ago. During this time ocean plates collided rapidly with the North American Plate. The Juan de Fuca Plate is all that is left of these ocean plates. Throughout this long time the western side of North America would have looked much like the Andes today.

Looking at the results of this in detail, we find that the Coast Ranges of the West Coast are made of folded and faulted slices of oceanic crust and some thin sedimentary rocks that were scraped off the ocean plate at the trench where the plate subducted. The Olympic Mountains in northwestern Washington

(Below) A map of North America showing the North American Cordillera in the west (Rockies, Sierra Nevada, Coast Ranges).

(Below) A simplified cross section through the cordillera of the western United States with the vertical scale greatly exaggerated.

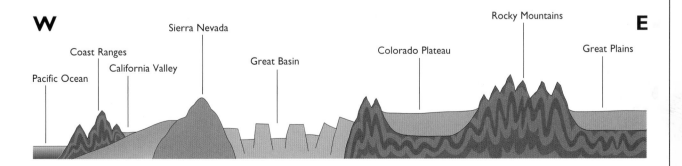

W — Pacific Ocean — Coast Ranges — California Valley — Sierra Nevada — Great Basin — Colorado Plateau — Rocky Mountains — Great Plains — E

are relic seamounts from the ancient ocean floor. Here you find metamorphosed ocean-floor basalt turned into serpentine. Unusually for a metamorphic rock, it is a weak material and explains why the Coast Ranges are readily eroded, subject to landslides, and have relatively gentle slopes.

The Sierra Nevada and western Canadian Rockies are made predominantly of granite. They mark a subduction zone that occurred between 170 million and 70 million years ago. Mount Whitney, the highest peak in the contiguous United States, is formed of granite from this subduction zone.

To the east of the subduction zone sedimentary rock was folded and faulted on the edge of the continental plate. This has given rise to the high ranges that are found in the Banff and Jasper National

(Below) The characteristic granite peaks of the Sierra Nevada. This is Yosemite, California.

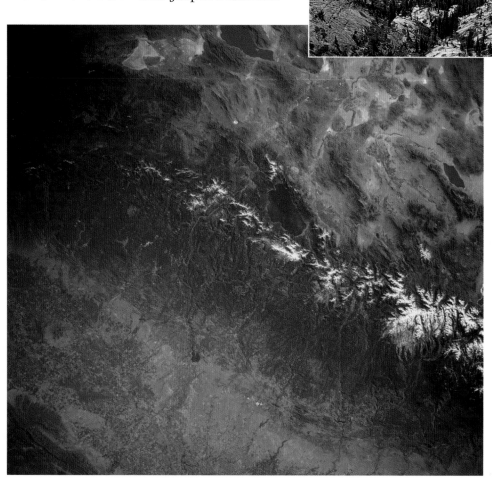

(Left) The Sierra Nevada in the area of Lake Tahoe.

(Left) Curving ranges of the Canadian Rockies as seen from the Space Shuttle.

(Below) The Canadian Rockies as seen from the ground.

Parks of the Canadian Rockies.

Beginning about 80 million years ago, the crust began to compress to the east of where the earlier activity had occurred. This caused great blocks of the continental crust to be thrust up to form the Front Range and also brought Precambrian-aged shield rocks up to the surface. They form the majority of the Rocky Mountains in the United States.

Between the Sierra subduction zone and the Rockies the land was changed very little, which is why the Colorado Plateau is so strikingly different from lands on either side.

The landscape of the Cordillera has been modified greatly since the last mountains were formed. For example, the continent has stretched to almost double its previous width, causing rift valleys to form, and leaving the block mountains and basins of the Great Basin and the Basin and Range areas.

It seems that under the western part of North America there has been considerable heating in the mantle, responsible for the many outbursts of volcanic material in the area, the stretching of the crust, and the elevation of the mountains to their present heights.

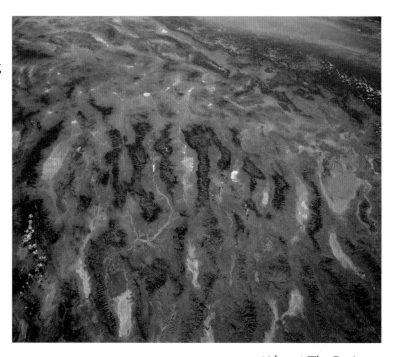

(Above) The Basin and Range region of the southwestern United States. This picture is taken from the Space Shuttle.

(Left) The Front Range of the Rockies near Denver as seen from space. The picture looks southwest, with the Front Range near the top right. Notice the sharp junction between the High Plains on which Denver is built and the Front Range, with its snow-capped peaks.

Continent-continent collision zones

When two continents collide, neither is pushed down into the mantle because the continental rocks are relatively light, and like two colliding icebergs, neither can move completely under the other. As a result, the crust crushes and thickens in the process.

This type of collision produces the most intense folding, faulting, heating, and metamorphic activity seen anywhere in the world, and it also produces the world's biggest and grandest mountains. The Himalayas, reaching to 8,854 meters at Mount Everest, form the highest continental mountains in the world. To the north of them the Tibetan Plateau is about 4,600 meters above sea level, higher than most of the Alps and almost all of the Rocky Mountains.

(Above) Continent-continent collisions.

Stages of collision

Seas surround the continents. Sediment carried from the land by rivers is deposited in these seas, often in the deep ocean troughs called geosynclines. These sediments form layers of sedimentary rock.

Geosynclines can lie hidden below the sea for tens or even hundreds of millions of years, slowly buckling down and appearing as nothing more than a piece of shallow seabed called a CONTINENTAL SHELF. The continental shelf off the east coast of North America is the top of a geosyncline, for example.

Geosynclines fill up with sediments while the crust below stays in one piece. But when plates begin to collide, the rocks below the geosyncline start to subduct below the continent. This begins a long process of mountain building.

First, the rocks in the geosyncline begin to buckle into folds. During this time the ocean plate on which they were forming slides under the continent. As the collision nears, the ocean floor is completely consumed, and one continent approaches another.

If the plates are moving very quickly, as is the case, for example, with India pushing into Asia, one plate may force its way below the other, at least for a while. In this case the rocks on the top of the plate that is underthrusting are scraped off and plastered onto the edge of the other continent.

The distance that these scraped-off pieces can be moved is very large, sometimes several hundred kilometers. The displaced pieces of crust are called NAPPES, and they dominate the mountains of belts like the Alps and the Himalayas.

Away from the point of collision the pressures on the layers of rock are less severe, and the sediments on the edge of the plate may simply be concertinaed, making a pattern of simple, regularly spaced folds, known as FOLD BELTS. The Valley and Ridge area of Pennsylvania in the Appalachian Mountains of eastern North America and the Jura Mountains on the northwestern side of the Alps are like this.

During collision the edge of the continent thickens and contains parts of the old plate as well as buckled sedimentary rocks. The old plates are made of metamorphic and IGNEOUS rocks that are much harder than the new sedimentary rocks, and so they withstand erosion to form the highest of the mountain rocks. The Himalayas, for example, are crystalline rocks formed by the collision. Here the rocks

(Above) The Alpine mountain-building belt north of the Mediterranean Sea.

(Below) Intensely folded rocks from the Swiss Alps.

occur in a confused pattern, and rarely is there a simple relationship between rocks and landscape, as there is in the folded regions to each side.

Old mountains made new again

Many very old mountain ranges were worn down to plains long ago. But these old mountains can be built into new mountain ranges. Examples that we can see today include the Appalachians of North America, the Caledonian Mountains of northern Europe, the Snowy Mountains of Australia, and all the mountains of Antarctica.

Their present heights are due to recent uplift because of heating and expansion of the mantle below the crust for reasons that, so far, no one understands.

(Below) Hard rocks that form steep, storm-resistant cliffs occur along much of the coast of northwestern Europe. The resistance of the rocks is due to the regional metamorphism they experienced during Caledonian and Hercynian times.

The Appalachian and Caledonian Mountains

The Appalachians (and their counterparts in Europe, the Caledonian and Hercynian Mountains that stretch from Scotland to the top of Norway and from southwestern England through central Europe) are a result of the collision of North America and Europe during the Early Paleozoic era.

(Below) A simplified cross section of the Appalachian Mountains with the vertical scale greatly exaggerated.

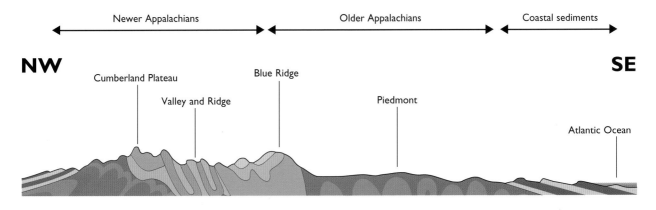

Newer Appalachians · Older Appalachians · Coastal sediments

NW

Cumberland Plateau · Valley and Ridge · Blue Ridge · Piedmont · Atlantic Ocean

SE

For perhaps a hundred million years, since CAMBRIAN times, sediment eroded from even earlier continents had built up in geosynclines in the ocean floor. Then the continents moved close enough for the ocean plate to be consumed into the mantle, and for the geosyncline to be crushed and its crushed rocks lifted to make the Appalachian/Caledonian mountains.

The earliest part of the collision was in the north, and the core of the huge mountain chain that was formed lay from New England through eastern Canada and Scotland into Norway. Later, South America and Africa also collided with North America, forming the southern Appalachians and the Hercynian-aged mountains of central Europe (and at the same time completing the gathering of the continents into the supercontinent called Pangaea).

(Above) A map of North America showing the Appalachians.

(Left) When seen from space, the Ridge and Valley region of the Pennsylvania Appalachians shows symmetrical folding.

(Below) The Caledonian Mountains of Scotland represent a part of the mountain system that was intensively folded and metamorphosed.

(Above) The Adirondacks are a part of the Canadian Shield (see page 56) lodged against the Appalachian Mountains. This view from space shows the way that glaciers have gouged valleys in which lakes now lie.

(Below) The famous Pass of Glencoe, Scotland, has many features typical of ancient mountain systems. The rugged mountains are all made from ancient volcanic rocks, mainly rhyolite.

(Above) The Caledonian Mountains of Europe.

The Alpine and Himalayan chains

The Himalayas and the Alps are all part of one enormous system of mountains that formed as Africa and India moved north and began to collide with Eurasia about 40 million years ago. Except for a few small fragments that have become bound up in the mountain ranges, the whole of the ocean floor that once existed between the two landmasses has been consumed back into the mantle.

This is a very good example of how collision causes rocks to be thrust over the continental margins as well as crumpled up between them.

The geosyncline that was squashed between the plates formed under an ocean that geologists call Tethys. However, the mountains that eventually replaced this ocean did not form at the same time or in the same way. The Alps, the Himalayas, and the mountains between them are all different in character.

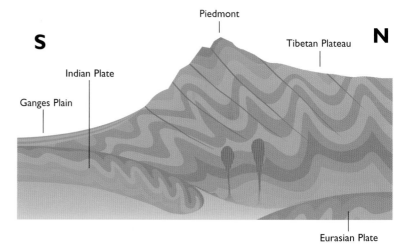

(Below) The formation of the Himalayas as a result of the collision of the Indian Plate with the Eurasian Plate.

(Below) Looking west across the Himalayas, with the Tibetan Plateau on the right and the Ganges Valley on the left.

So far India has moved 2,000 kilometers into the flank of Asia. The Himalayas are made of the upper slice of the Indian plate, which is gradually scraping its rocks off as it moves under the Asian Plate. At present this process is making the Himalayas rise by more than 1 centimeter a year, or by 10 kilometers in a million years.

There is a huge thrust fault lying below the Himalayas. As India pushes into Asia, the Himalayas are pushed south on top of this fault. This is where the rocks from deep in the crust are carried up to the surface to make the world's highest mountains.

Most of the rocks of the Himalayas are metamorphic and come from the middle and lower crust of India's ancient northern edge. The very tops of many of the peaks, by contrast, are made of sedimentary rocks representing the last remains of the ancient Tethys Ocean sediments

(Above) The Himalayas.

(Below) Mount Everest in the Himalayan ranges of the Asian cordillera.

that were carried on top of the crumpling edge of the Indian Plate.

To the north of the Himalayas lies the great Tibetan Plateau, itself a region of folded rocks buried by sediments eroded from the Himalayas so that it appears to be a plain. To the north again lies the Tien Shan region, with peaks above 7,000 meters in height. It is an area of great block faulting lifted up at the same time as the Himalayas.

Further west, Arabia collided with southern Iran and Turkey, creating the same pattern of mountains on a much smaller scale.

The Alps, which are the most westerly part of this mountain system, are the most complicated.

The Alpine mountain system formed as a result of Africa moving north into Europe. Again, a geosyncline was crumpled up. The leading part of Africa was a promontory that now makes the "boot" of Italy. It has forged ahead, forcing the Alps to curve around it.

In this case it is Europe that began to push under Africa, the reverse of the case with the Himalayas. As Europe was forced under Italy and the rest of Africa,

(Below) The northern part of Italy and Slovenia (part of the African Plate) looking northeastward to where it has pushed into the southern flank of Europe.

(Below) A simplified cross section of the Alps showing how huge folds (nappes) were created during mountain building. The vertical scale is greatly exaggerated.

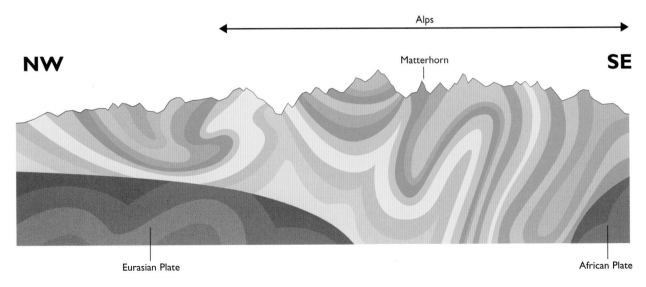

NW

SE

Alps

Matterhorn

Eurasian Plate

African Plate

it thrust up great sheets of rock onto the more stable parts of Europe to the north. Huge thrust faults and folds were formed, and rocks driven hundreds of kilometers from their roots formed large nappes.

At the same time, Italy scraped up bits and pieces of the deeper metamorphic rocks of Europe's ancient plate. As a result, while the northernmost parts of the Alps are made of folded unmetamorphosed rocks, the southern parts are nearly all metamorphic rocks.

Parts of the Mediterranean Sea still represent the last remnants of the Tethys Ocean.

(Below) The Jura (left) and Alps (right), with Lake Geneva occupying the Swiss Plain between them.

(Below) The Swiss Alps, looking north in the direction that the nappes were thrust.

Transform (sliding) plate boundaries

When two plates slide past one another, the fault is called a transform fault (see page 28). Most of these faults occur in the ocean floors, but a few occur on land, the largest of which is the San Andreas Fault Zone in California. This transform fault connects the East Pacific Rise, a spreading boundary to the south, with the South Gorda-Juan de Fuca-Explorer Ridge, another spreading boundary to the north.

The San Andreas Fault Zone is about 1,300 kilometers long and in places tens of kilometers wide. It is found through two-thirds of the length of California. Here the western edge of California slips northward with respect to the mainland at a rate of about five centimeters a year. This kind of boundary produces many earthquakes, but no significant landscape features.

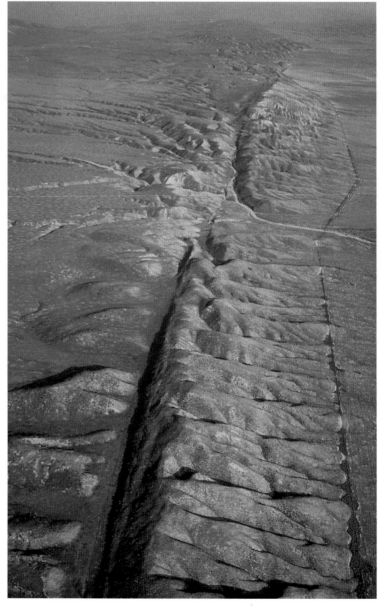

(Below) Aerial view of the San Andreas Fault slicing through the Carrizo Plain in the Temblor Range east of the city of San Luis Obispo.

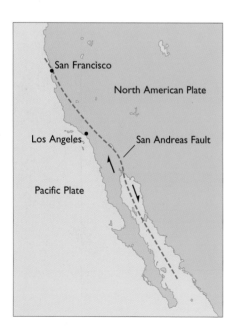

(Above) A transform fault runs almost all the way along the western boundary of North America.

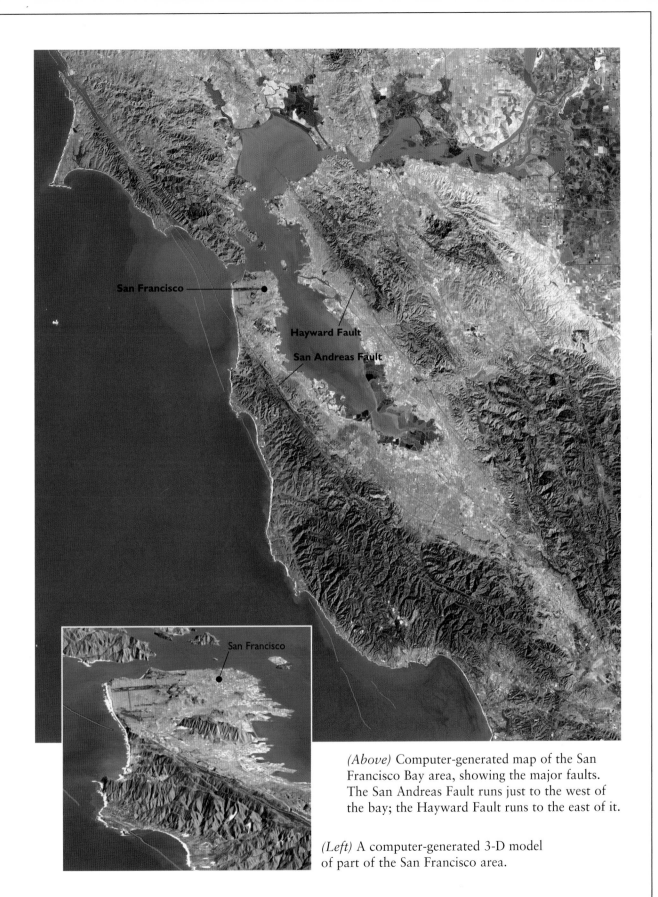

San Francisco

Hayward Fault

San Andreas Fault

San Francisco

(Above) Computer-generated map of the San Francisco Bay area, showing the major faults. The San Andreas Fault runs just to the west of the bay; the Hayward Fault runs to the east of it.

(Left) A computer-generated 3-D model of part of the San Francisco area.

Chapter 4: Shields and hot spots

The main places where changes occur are at plate boundaries. But although the middles of plates are places where little is happening, special areas called hot spots can produce violent activity right in the ancient centers of plates.

Shields

The centers of the great continental plates are immensely old. They are the most stable parts of the earth's crust and are called SHIELDS, or CRATONS.

Some parts of these rocks in Australia and South Africa can be dated back at least 3.9 billion years, and all shields have an average age of 2.3 billion years—half the age of the earth.

Shields are the worn-down remains of old mountain systems. Some probably represent the remains of the first fold mountain systems ever to rise on the earth.

The first mountains were probably volcanic. When they were eroded, they produced sediments that built up in the seas nearby. When the ancient plates collided, it was these sediments that were buckled up into fold mountains on the edges of the plates. The sediments are less dense than the volcanic basalts from which they were formed, and so they have remained afloat on the plates ever since.

(Below) The shields have formed by the addition (accretion) of new fold mountains at their edges. The centers of the plates are thus often the oldest parts of the plate, with rocks becoming progressively younger toward the plate edges.

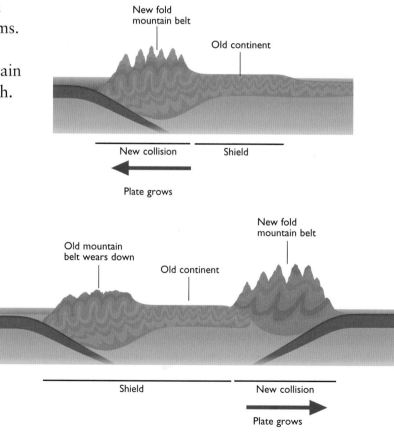

New fold mountain belt

Old continent

New collision Shield

Plate grows

Old mountain belt wears down

Old continent

New fold mountain belt

Shield New collision

Plate grows

As each new collision created more mountains on the sides of these first plates, the plates grew. This is called **MARGINAL ACCRETION**. Thus, although the shield areas were once small, they are now large and still growing.

The land of these shields typically contains the remains of many old mountain systems. They are made of igneous rocks such as granite and intensely metamorphosed and folded rocks such as gneisses. All are crystalline and very hard.

(Below) Africa is made almost entirely of shield-type continent. Most of this shield has been land since **ORDOVICIAN** times. The cape region of southern Africa lies on the shield. This picture from space looks across the Kalahari Desert to Cape Town. There are no fold mountains at all in this area.

The wreckage of all kinds of mountain building and subduction can be found in these shields. There are remains of fold mountains and island arcs as well as the folded sediments that once formed in geosynclines and the BATHOLITHS that were produced as magma forced its way into the subducted rocks.

The shields are not thick because they have been worn down by long periods of erosion. As a result, they can be split, and this has happened several times in the past, as with the supercontinent called Pangaea.

There are shields in all the continents. Africa and Australia are the continents where shields are most visible at the surface, and where they occupy the majority of the land. In North America the Canadian Shield occupies the northeast of the continent at the surface, but shields underlie the land as far west as the Rocky Mountains. In South America the main shield, the Brazilian Shield, underlies the Amazon Basin, with another called the Guyana Shield to the north of it.

(Above) The area of North America in which the Canadian Shield (shown dark green on this map) can still be found on the surface.

(Right) Australia, showing the location of Western Australia and the Hamersley Range.

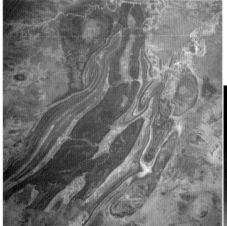

(Above and right) These near-vertical views from space allow us to see fascinating patterns in the rocks of a large region of Western Australia.

The Hamersley Range in Western Australia lies in the Australian Shield. The oval shapes are the tops of Precambrian batholiths that now mark the line of these ancient mountains.

In Europe the Baltic Shield lies to the east of the Scandinavian Mountains, stretching eastward under Russia. Another shield lies under Siberia.

In southern and eastern Asia there are three more shields, the Angara, the Chinese, and the Indian. Between them stretch the mountain chains that include the Himalayas, the Alps, and the Urals.

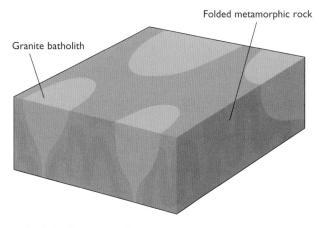

Granite batholith

Folded metamorphic rock

(Right) Continental shields were once mountain ranges that had mountain roots. As the mountains were eroded, ISOSTACY caused the roots to rise, keeping the mountains quite high for very long periods. However, this was at the expense of the thickness of the crust.

Shields finally wear down to low-lying land, and the crust is therefore relatively thin (top diagram). From time to time sea levels can rise, or whole areas of the plate can sink. This allows the land to be flooded and sediments to be deposited as thin sheets. When the land rises again, the soft sedimentary rocks are eroded away, sometimes leaving isolated hills (bottom diagram).

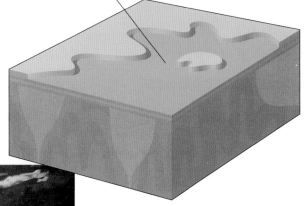

Eroded sedimentary rocks

Ayers Rock

(Left) Ayers Rock in Australia is a remnant of layers of sedimentary rocks that cover the Australian Shield. No mountain building has affected this area since Precambrian times, although the shields have, from time to time, been covered by shallow seas. This is when the sediments were laid down that have subsequently been eroded into Ayers Rock.

Hot spots

One of the curious features of the way that magma rises to the surface is its appearance in isolated places across the earth. While most of the magma rises in well-marked zones (where plates spread apart or where they push together), there are some long-lasting places where magma appears to rise quite independently of the plates. They are known as hot spots. Plates ride across them, and in some cases the hot spot plumes may be powerful enough to break up the plates. It is just possible that hot spots could have caused the breakup of supercontinents in the past.

Over a hundred hot spots have been found that have been active during the last 10 million years. One of the world's most prominent hot spots lies in the Pacific Ocean and is marked by the chain of volcanoes that make up the Hawaiian Islands. Not all hot spots appear in the oceans; some also form in the interiors of continental plates. The domed landscape of the East African Rift Valley area may be a current example. Yellowstone National Park, with its famous geysers, may be located over another continental hot spot.

Hot spots may also be the source of the massive eruptions of lava known as flood basalts, which can send out lava covering thousands of square kilometers. Examples of such flood basalts are the Columbia-Snake River area in the northwestern United States and the Deccan Traps of central India.

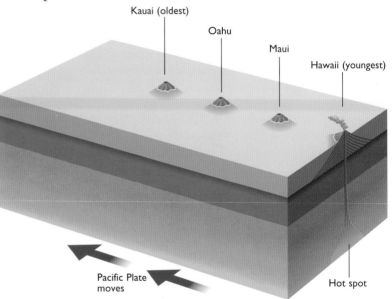

(Below) The relationship of the Hawaiian Islands to a hot spot.

Kauai (oldest)

Oahu

Maui

Hawaii (youngest)

Pacific Plate moves

Hot spot

(*Right and below*) Many of the seamounts in the oceans are probably volcanoes that were once created by hot spots.

The most famous active hot spot lies in the Pacific Ocean. It is clearly a very deep-seated feature, for it remains stationary while the Pacific Ocean floor spreads across it. As a result, rising magma continues to puncture the ocean crust, producing the string of volcanoes that make up the Hawaiian Islands.

➤ The Hawaiian Islands are more than 3,200 kilometers from the nearest plate boundary.

The oldest volcanic rocks are on the northwesternmost Hawaiian island. They are about 5.5 million years old. The youngest of the islands is the "Big Island" of Hawaii (shown on the right), and its rocks are less than 0.7 million years old.

The more detailed space picture below shows part of Mauna Loa, with a long fissure running across its summit. Old lava flows can be seen on either side of the fissure. The white smoke plume is from the summit of Kilauea, and the white steam plume shows where hot lava reaches the sea.

Glossary

aa lava: a type of lava with a broken, bouldery surface.

abrasion: the rubbing away (erosion) of a rock by the physical scraping of particles carried by water, wind, or ice.

acidic rock: a type of igneous rock that consists predominantly of light-colored minerals and more than two-thirds silica (e.g., granite).

active volcano: a volcano that has observable signs of activity, for example, periodic plumes of steam.

adit: a horizontal tunnel drilled into rock.

aftershock: an earthquake that follows the main shock. Major earthquakes are followed by a number of aftershocks that decrease in frequency with time.

agglomerate: a rock made from the compacted particles thrown out by a volcano (e.g., tuff).

alkaline rock: a type of igneous rock containing less than half silica and normally dominated by dark-colored minerals (e.g., gabbro).

amygdule: a vesicle in a volcanic rock filled with such secondary minerals such as calcite, quartz, or zeolite.

andesite: an igneous volcanic rock. Slightly more acidic than basalt.

anticline: an arching fold of rock layers in which the rocks slope down from the crest. *See also* syncline.

Appalachian Mountain (Orogenic) Belt: an old mountain range that extends for more than 3,000 km along the eastern margin of North America from Alabama in the southern United States to Newfoundland, Canada, in the north. There were three Appalachian orogenies: Taconic (about 460 million years ago) in the Ordovician; Acadian (390 to 370 million years ago) in the Devonian; and Alleghenian (300 to 250 million years ago) in the Late Carboniferous to Permian. These mountain belts can be traced as the Caledonian and Hercynian orogenic belts in Europe.

Archean Eon: *see* eon.

arenaceous: a rock composed largely of sand grains.

argillaceous: a rock composed largely of clay.

arkose: a coarse sandstone formed by the disintegration of a granite.

ash, volcanic: fine powdery material thrown out of a volcano.

asthenosphere: the weak part of the upper mantle below the lithosphere, in which slow convection is thought to take place.

augite: a dark green-colored silicate mineral containing calcium, sodium, iron, aluminum, and magnesium.

axis of symmetry: a line or plane around which one part of a crystal is a mirror image of another part.

basalt: basic fine-grained igneous volcanic rock; lava often contains vesicles.

basic rock: an igneous rock (e.g., gabbro) with silica content less than two-thirds and containing a high percentage of dark-colored minerals.

basin: a large, circular, or oval sunken region on the earth's surface created by downward folding. A river basin, or watershed, is the area drained by a river and its tributaries.

batholith: a very large body of plutonic rock that was intruded deep into the earth's crust and is now exposed by erosion.

bauxite: a surface material that contains a high percentage of aluminum silicate. The principal ore of aluminum.

bed: a layer of sediment. It may involve many phases of deposition, each marked by a bedding plane.

bedding plane: an ancient surface on which sediment built up. Sedimentary rocks often split along bedding planes.

biotite: a black-colored form of mica.

body wave: a seismic wave that can travel through the interior of the earth. P waves and S waves are body waves.

boss: an upward extension of a batholith. A boss may once have been a magma chamber.

botryoidal: the shape of a mineral that resembles a bunch of grapes, e.g., hematite whose crystals are often arranged in massive clumps, giving a surface covered with spherical bulges.

butte: a small mesa.

calcareous: composed mainly of calcium carbonate.

calcite: a mineral composed of calcium carbonate.

caldera: the collapsed cone of a volcano. It sometimes contains a crater lake.

Caledonian Mountain-Building Period, Caledonian Orogeny: a major mountain-building period in the Lower Paleozoic Era that reached its climax at the end of the Silurian Period (430 to 395 million years ago). An early phase affected only North America and made part of the Appalachian Mountain Belt.

Cambrian, Cambrian Period: the first period of geological time in the Paleozoic Era, beginning 570 million years ago and ending 500 million years ago.

carbonate minerals: minerals formed with carbonate ions (e.g., calcite).

Carboniferous, Carboniferous Period: a period of geological time between about 345 and 280 million years ago. It is often divided into the Early Carboniferous Epoch (345 to 320 million years ago) and the Late Carboniferous Epoch (320 to 280 million years ago). The Late Carboniferous is characterized by large coal-forming swamps. In North America the Carboniferous is usually divided into the Mississippian (= Lower Carboniferous) and Pennsylvanian (= Upper Carboniferous) periods.

cast, fossil: the natural filling of a mold by sediment or minerals that were left when a fossil dissolved after being enclosed by rock.

Cenozoic, Cenozoic Era: the most recent era of geological time, beginning 65 million years ago and continuing to the present.

central vent volcano: *see* stratovolcano

chemical compound: a substance made from the chemical combination of two or more elements.

chemical rock: a rock produced by chemical precipitation (e.g., halite).

chemical weathering: the decay of a rock through the chemical action of water containing dissolved acidic gases.

cinder cone: a volcanic cone made entirely of cinders. Cinder cones have very steep sides.

class: the level of biological classification below a phylum.

clast: an individual grain of a rock.

clastic rock: a sedimentary rock that is made up of fragments of preexisting rocks, carried by gravity, water, or wind (e.g., conglomerate, sandstone).

cleavage: the tendency of some minerals to break along one or more smooth surfaces.

coal: the carbon-rich, solid mineral derived from fossilized plant remains. Found in sedimentary rocks. Types of coal include bituminous, brown, lignite, and anthracite. A fossil fuel.

complex volcano: a volcano that has had an eruptive history that produces two or more vents.

composite volcano: *see* stratovolcano.

concordant coast: a coast where the geological structure is parallel to the coastline. *See also* discordant coastline.

conduction (of heat): the transfer of heat between touching objects.

conglomerate: a coarse-grained sedimentary rock with grains larger than 2 mm.

contact metamorphism: metamorphism that occurs due to direct contact with a molten magma. *See also* regional metamorphism.

continental drift: the theory suggested by Alfred Wegener that earth's continents were originally one land mass that split up to form the arrangement of continents we see today.

continental shelf: the ocean floor from the coastal shore of continents to the continental slope.

continental shield: the ancient and stable core of a tectonic plate. Also called a shield.

convection: the slow overturning of a liquid or gas that is heated from below.

cordillera: a long mountain belt consisting of many mountain ranges.

core: the innermost part of the earth. The earth's core is very dense, rich in iron, partly molten, and the source of the earth's magnetic field. The inner core is solid and has a radius of about 1,300 kilometers. The outer core is fluid and is about 2,100 kilometers thick. S waves cannot travel through the outer core.

cracking: the breaking up of a hydrocarbon compound into simpler constituents by means of heat.

crater lake: a lake found inside a caldera.

craton: *see* shield.

Cretaceous, Cretaceous Period: the third period of the Mesozoic Era. It lasted between about 135 and 65 million years ago. It was a time of chalk formation and when many dinosaurs lived.

cross-bedding: a pattern of deposits in a sedimentary rock in which many thin layers lie at an angle to the bedding planes, showing that the sediment was deposited by a moving fluid. Wind-deposited cross-beds are often bigger than water-deposited beds.

crust: the outermost layer of the earth, typically 5 km under the oceans and 50 to 100 km thick under continents. It makes up less than 1 percent of the earth's volume.

crustal plate: *see* tectonic plate.

crystal: a mineral that has a regular geometric shape and is bounded by smooth, flat faces.

crystal system: a group of crystals with the same arrangement of axes.

crystalline: a mineral that has solidified but been unable to produce well-formed crystals. Quartz and halite are commonly found as crystalline masses.

crystallization: the formation of crystals.

cubic: a crystal system in which crystals have 3 axes all at right angles to one another and of equal length.

cuesta: a ridge in the landscape formed by a resistant band of dipping rock. A cuesta has a steep scarp slope and a more gentle dip slope.

current bedding: a pattern of deposits in a sedimentary rock in which many thin layers lie at an angle to the bedding planes, showing that the sediment was deposited by a current of water.

cyclothem: a repeating sequence of rocks found in coal strata.

delta: a triangle of deposition produced where a river enters a sea or lake.

deposit, deposition: the process of laying down material that has been transported in suspension or solution by water, ice, or wind. A deposit is the material laid down by deposition (e.g., salt deposits).

destructive plate boundary: a line where plates collide and one plate is subducted into the mantle.

Devonian, Devonian Period: the fourth period of geological time in the Paleozoic Era from 395 to 345 million years ago.

dike: a wall-like sheet of igneous rock that cuts across the layers of the surrounding rocks.

dike swarm: a collection of hundreds or thousands of parallel dikes.

diorite: an igneous plutonic rock between gabbro and granite; the plutonic equivalent of andesite.

dip: the angle that a bedding plane or fault makes with the horizontal.

dip slope: the more gently sloping part of a cuesta whose surface often parallels the dip of the strata.

discontinuity: a gap in deposition, perhaps caused by the area being lifted above the sea so that erosion, rather than deposition, occurred for a time.

discordant coast: a coast where the rock structure is at an angle to the line of the coast. *See also* concordant coastline.

displacement: the distance that one piece of rock is pushed relative to another.

dissolve: to break down a substance into a solution without causing a reaction.

distillation: the boiling off of volatile materials, leaving a residue.

dolomite: a mineral composed of calcium magnesium carbonate.

dome: a circular uplifted region of rocks taking the shape of a dome and found in some areas of folded rocks. Rising plugs of salt will also dome up the rocks above them. They sometimes make oil traps.

dormant volcano: a volcano that shows no signs of activity but that has been active in the recent past.

drift: a tunnel drilled in rock and designed to provide a sloping route for carrying out ore or coal by means of a conveyor belt.

earthquake: shaking of the earth's surface caused by a sudden movement of rock within the earth.

element: a fundamental chemical building block. A substance that cannot be separated into simpler substances by any chemical means. Oxygen and sulfur are examples of elements.

eon: the largest division of geological time. An eon is subdivided into eras. Precambrian time is divided into the Archean (earlier than 2.5 billion years ago) and Proterozoic eons (more recent than 2.5 billion years ago). The Phanerozoic Eon includes the Cambrian Period to the present.

epicenter: the point on the earth's surface directly above the focus (hypocenter) of an earthquake.

epoch: a subdivision of a geological period in the geological time scale (e.g., Pleistocene Epoch).

era: a subdivision of a geological eon in the geological time scale (e.g., Cenozoic Era). An era is subdivided into periods.

erode, erosion: the twin processes of breaking down a rock (called weathering) and then removing the debris (called transporting).

escarpment: the crest of a ridge made of dipping rocks.

essential mineral: the dominant mineral constituents of a rock used to classify it.

evaporite: a mineral or rock formed as the result of evaporation of salt-laden water, such as a lagoon or salt lake.

exoskeleton: another word for shell. Applies to invertebrates.

extinct volcano: a volcano that has shown no signs of activity in historic times.

extrusive rock, extrusion: an igneous volcanic rock that has solidified on the surface of the earth.

facet: the cleaved face of a mineral. Used in describing jewelry.

facies: physical, chemical, or biological variations in a sedimentary bed of the same geological age (e.g., sandy facies, limestone facies).

family: a part of the classification of living things above a genus.

fault: a deep fracture or zone of fractures in rocks along which there has been displacement of one side relative to the other. It represents a weak point in the crust and upper mantle.

fault scarp: a long, straight, steep slope in the landscape that has been produced by faulting.

feldspar: the most common silicate mineral. It consists of two forms: plagioclase and orthoclase.

ferromagnesian mineral: dark-colored minerals such as augite and hornblende that contain relatively high proportions of iron and magnesium and low proportions of silica.

fissure: a substantial crack in a rock.

fjord: a glaciated valley in a mountainous area coastal area that has been partly flooded by the sea.

focal depth: the depth of an earthquake focus below the surface.

focus: the origin of an earthquake, directly below the epicenter.

fold: arched or curved rock strata.

fold axis: line following the highest arching in an anticline or the lowest arching in a syncline.

fold belt: a part of a mountain system containing folded sedimentary rocks.

foliation: a texture of a rock (usually schist) that resembles the pages in a book.

formation: a word used to describe a collection of related rock layers, or beds. A number of related beds make a member; a collection of related members makes up a formation. Formations are often given location names, e.g., Toroweap Formation, whose members are a collection of dominantly limestone beds.

fossil: any evidence of past life, including remains, traces, and imprints.

fossil fuel: any fuel that was formed in the geological past from the remains of living organisms. The main fossil fuels are coal and petroleum (oil and natural gas).

fraction: one of the components of crude oil that can be separated from others by heating and then cooling the vapor.

fracture: a substantial break across a rock.

fracture zone: a region in which fractures are common. Fracture zones are particularly common in folded rock and near faults.

frost shattering: the process of breaking pieces of rock through the action of freezing and melting of rainwater

gabbro: alkaline igneous plutonic rock, typically showing dark-colored crystals; plutonic equivalent of basalt.

gallery: a horizontal access tunnel in a mine.

gangue: the unwanted mineral matter found in association with a metal.

gem: a mineral, usually in crystal form, that is regarded as having particular beauty and value.

genus: (*pl.* genera) the biological classification for a group of closely related species.

geode: a hollow lump of rock (nodule) that often contains crystals.

geological column: a columnar diagram showing the divisions of geological time (eons, eras, periods, and epochs).

geological eon: *see* eon.

geological epoch: *see* epoch.

geological era: *see* era.

geological period: a subdivision of a geological era (e.g., Carboniferous Period). A period is subdivided into epochs.

geological system: a term for an accumulation of strata that occurs during a geological period (e.g., the Ordovician System is the rocks deposited during the Ordovician Period). Systems are divided into series.

geological time: the history of the earth revealed by its rocks.

geological time scale: the division of geological time into eons, era, periods, and epochs.

geosyncline: a large, slowly subsiding region marginal to a continent where huge amounts of sediment accumulate. The rocks in a geosyncline eventually are lifted to form mountain belts.

gneiss: a metamorphic rock showing large grains.

graben: a fallen block of the earth's crust forming a long trough separated on all sides by faults. Associated with rift valleys.

grain: a particle of a rock or mineral.

granite: an acidic, igneous, plutonic rock containing free quartz, typically light in color; plutonic equivalent of rhyolite.

grit: grains larger than sand but smaller than stones.

groundmass: *see* matrix.

group: a word used to describe a collection of related rock layers, or beds. A number of related beds make a member; a collection of related members makes up a formation; a collection of related formations makes a group.

gypsum: a mineral made of calcium sulfate.

halide minerals: a group of minerals (e.g., halite) that contain a halogen element (elements similar to chlorine) bonded with another element. Many are evaporite minerals.

halite: a mineral made of sodium chloride.

Hawaiian-type eruption: a name for a volcanic eruption that mainly consists of lava fountains.

hexagonal: a crystal system in which crystals have 3 axes all at 120 degrees to one another and of equal length.

hogback: a cuesta where the scarp and dip slopes are about the same angle.

hornblende: a dark-green silicate mineral of the amphibole group containing sodium, potassium, calcium, magnesium, iron, and aluminum.

horst: a raised block of the earth's crust separated on all sides by faults. Associated with rift valleys.

hot spot: a place where a fixed mantle magma plume reaches the surface.

hydraulic action: the erosive action of water pressure on rocks.

hydrothermal: a change brought about in a rock or mineral due to the action of superheated mineral-rich fluids, usually water.

hypocenter: the calculated location of the focus of an earthquake.

ice wedging: *see* frost shattering

Icelandic-type eruption: a name given to a fissure type of eruption.

igneous rock: rock formed by the solidification of magma. Igneous rocks include volcanic and plutonic rocks.

impermeable: a rock that will not allow a liquid to pass through it.

imprint: a cast left by a former life form.

impurities: small amounts of elements or compounds in an otherwise homogeneous mineral.

index fossil: a fossil used as a marker for a particular part of geological time.

intrusive rock, intrusion: rocks that have formed from cooling magma below the surface. When inserted among other rocks, intruded rocks are called an intrusion.

invertebrate: an animal with an external skeleton.

ion: a charged particle.

island arc: a pattern of volcanic islands that follow the shape of an arc when seen from above.

isostacy: the principle that a body can float in a more dense fluid. The same as buoyancy, but used for continents.

joint: a significant crack between blocks of rock, normally used in the context of patterns of cracks.

Jurassic, Jurassic Period: the second geological period in the Mesozoic Era, lasting between 190 and 135 million years ago.

kingdom: the broadest division in the biological classification of living things.

laccolith: a lens-shaped body of intrusive igneous rock with a dome-shaped upper surface and a flat bottom surface.

landform: a recognizable shape of part of the landscape, for example, a cuesta.

landslide: the rapid movement of a slab of soil down a steep hillslope.

lateral fault: *see* thrust fault.

laterite: a surface deposit containing a high proportion of iron.

lava: molten rock material extruded onto the surface of the earth.

lava bomb: *see* volcanic bomb.

law of superposition: the principle that younger rock is deposited on older.

limestone: a carbonate sedimentary rock composed of more than half calcium carbonate.

lithosphere: that part of the crust and upper mantle that is brittle and makes up the tectonic plates.

lode: a mining term for a rock containing many rich ore-bearing minerals. Similar to vein.

Love wave, L wave: a major type of surface earthquake wave that shakes the ground surface at right angles to the direction the wave is traveling in. It is named after A.E.H. Love, the English mathematician who discovered it.

luster: the way in which a mineral reflects light. Used as a test when identifying minerals.

magma: the molten material that comes from the mantle and that cools to form igneous rocks.

magma chamber: a large cavity melted in the earth's crust and filled with magma. Many magma chambers are plumes of magma that have melted their way from the mantle to the upper part of the crust. When a magma chamber is no longer supplied with molten magma, the magma solidifies to form a granite batholith.

mantle: the layer of the earth between the crust and the core. It is approximately 2,900 kilometers thick and is the largest of the earth's major layers.

marginal accretion: the growth of mountain belts on the edges of a shield.

mass extinction: a time when the majority of species on the planet were killed off.

matrix: the rock or sediment in which a fossil is embedded; the fine-grained rock in which larger particles are embedded, for example, in a conglomerate.

mechanical weathering: the disintegration of a rock by frost shattering/ice wedging.

mesa: a large detached piece of a tableland.

Mesozoic, Mesozoic Era: the geological era between the Paleozoic and the Cenozoic eras. It lasted between 225 and 65 million years ago.

metamorphic aureole: the region of contact metamorphic rock that surrounds a batholith.

metamorphic rock: any rock (e.g., schist, gneiss) that was formed from a preexisting rock through heat and pressure.

meteorite: a substantial chunk of rock in space.

micas: a group of soft, sheetlike silicate minerals (e.g., biotite, muscovite).

midocean ridge: a long mountain chain on the ocean floor where basalt periodically erupts, forming new oceanic crust.

mineral: a naturally occurring inorganic substance of definite chemical composition (e.g., calcite, calcium carbonate).
More generally, any resource extracted from the ground by mining (includes, metal ores, coal, oil, gas, rocks, etc.).

mineral environment: the place where a mineral or a group of associated minerals forms. Mineral environments include igneous, sedimentary, and metamorphic rocks.

mineralization: the formation of minerals within a rock.

Modified Mercalli Scale: a scale for measuring the impact of an earthquake. It is composed of 12 increasing levels of intensity that range from imperceptible, designated by Roman numeral I, to catastrophic destruction, designated by XII.

Mohorovicic discontinuity: the boundary surface that separates the earth's crust from the underlying mantle. Named for Andrija Mohorovicic, a Croatian seismologist.

Mohs' Scale of Hardness: a relative scale developed to put minerals into an order. The hardest is 10 (diamond), and the softest is 1 (talc).

mold: an impression in a rock of the outside of an organism.

monoclinic: a crystal system in which crystals have 2 axes all at right angles to one another, and each axis is of unequal length.

mountain belt: a region where there are many ranges of mountains. The term is often applied to a wide belt of mountains produced during mountain building.

mountain building: the creation of mountains as a result of the collision of tectonic plates. Long belts or chains of mountains can form along the edge of a continent during this process. Mountain building is also called orogeny.

mountain-building period: a period during which a geosyncline is compressed into fold mountains by the collision of two tectonic plates. Also known as orogenesis.

mudstone: a fine-grained, massive rock formed by the compaction of mud.

nappe: a piece of a fold that has become detached from its roots during intensive mountain building.

native metal: a metal that occurs uncombined with any other element.

natural gas: *see* petroleum.

normal fault: a fault in which one block has slipped down the face of another. It is the most common kind of fault and results from tension.

nueé ardente: another word for pyroclastic flow.

ocean trench: a deep, steep-sided trough in the ocean floor caused by the subduction of oceanic crust beneath either other oceanic crust or continental crust.

olivine: the name of a group of magnesium iron silicate minerals that have an olive color.

order: a level of biological classification between class and family.

Ordovician, Ordovician Period: the second period of geological time within the Paleozoic Era. It lasted from 500 to 430 million years ago.

ore: a rock containing enough useful metal or fuel to be worth mining.

ore mineral: a mineral that occurs in sufficient quantity to be mined for its metal. The compound must also be easy to process.

organic rocks: rocks formed by living things, for example, coal.

orthoclase: the form of feldspar that is often pink in color and that contains potassium as important ions.

orogenic belt: a mountain belt.

orogeny: a period of mountain building. Orogenesis is the process of mountain building and the creation of orogenic belts.

orthorhombic: a crystal system in which crystals have 3 axes all at right angles to one another but of unequal length.

outcrop: the exposure of a rock at the surface of the earth.

overburden: the unwanted layer(s) of rock above an ore or coal body.

oxide minerals: a group of minerals in which oxygen is a major constituent. A compound in which oxygen is bonded to another element or group.

Pacific Ring of Fire: the ring of volcanoes and volcanic activity that circles the Pacific Ocean. Created by the collision of the Pacific Plate with its neighboring plates.

pahoehoe lava: the name for a form of lava that has a smooth surface.

Paleozoic, Paleozoic Era: a major interval of geological time. The Paleozoic is the oldest era in which fossil life is commonly found. It lasted from 570 to 225 million years ago.

paleomagnetism: the natural magnetic traces that reveal the intensity and direction of the earth's magnetic field in the geological past.

pegmatite: an igneous rock (e.g., a dike) of extremely coarse crystals.

Pelean-type eruption: a violent explosion dominated by pyroclastic flows.

period: *see* geological period.

permeable rock: a rock that will allow a fluid to pass through it.

Permian, Permian Period: the last period of the Paleozoic Era, lasting from 280 to 225 million years ago.

petrified: when the tissues of a dead plant or animal have been replaced by minerals, such as silica, they are said to be petrified (e.g., petrified wood).

petrified forest: a large number of fossil trees. Most petrified trees are replaced by silica.

petroleum: the carbon-rich, and mostly liquid, mixture produced by the burial and partial alteration of animal and plant remains. Petroleum is found in many sedimentary rocks. The liquid part of petroleum is called oil. The gaseous part of petroleum is known as natural gas. Petroleum is an important fossil fuel.

petroleum field: a region from which petroleum can be recovered.

Phanerozoic Eon: the most recent eon, beginning at the Cambrian Period, some 570 million years ago, and extending up to the present.

phenocryst: an especially large crystal (in a porphyritic rock) embedded in smaller mineral grains.

phylum: (*pl.* phyla) biological classification for one of the major divisions of animal life and second in complexity to kingdom. The plant kingdom is not divided into phyla but into divisions.

placer deposit: a sediment containing heavy metal grains (e.g., gold) that have weathered out of the bedrock and concentrated on a stream bed or along a coast.

plagioclase: the form of feldspar that is often white or gray and that contains sodium and calcium as important ions.

planetismals: small embryo planets.

plate: *see* plate tectonics, tectonic plate.

plateau: an extensive area of raised flat land. The clifflike edges of a plateau may, when eroded, leave isolated features such as mesas and buttes. *See also* tableland.

plate tectonics: the theory that the earth's crust and upper mantle (the lithosphere) are broken into a number of more or less rigid, but constantly moving, slabs or plates.

Plinian-type eruption: an explosive eruption that sends a column of ash high into the air.

plug: *see* volcanic plug

plunging fold: a fold whose axis dips, or plunges, into the ground.

plutonic rock: an igneous rock that has solidified at great depth and contains large crystals due to the slowness of cooling (e.g., granite, gabbro).

porphyry, porphyritic rock: an igneous rock in which larger crystals (phenocrysts) are enclosed in a fine-grained matrix.

Precambrian, Precambrian time: the whole of earth history before the Cambrian Period. Also called Precambrian Era and Precambrian Eon.

precipitate: a substance that has settled out of a liquid as a result of a chemical reaction between two chemicals in the liquid.

Primary Era: an older name for the Paleozoic Era.

prismatic: a word used to describe a mineral that has formed with one axis very much longer than the others.

Proterozoic Eon: *see* eon.

P wave, primary wave, primary seismic wave: P waves are the fastest body waves. The waves carry energy in the same line as the direction of the wave. P waves can travel through all layers of the earth and are generally felt as a thump. *See also* S wave.

pyrite: iron sulfide. It is common in sedimentary rocks that were poor in oxygen and sometimes forms fossil casts.

pyroclastic flow: solid material ejected from a volcano, combined with searing hot gases, which together behave as a high-density fluid. Pyroclastic flows can do immense damage, as was the case with Mount Saint Helens.

pyroclastic material: any solid material ejected from a volcano.

Quaternary, Quaternary Period: the second period in the Cenozoic Era, beginning about 1.6 million years ago and continuing to the present day.

radiation: the transfer of energy between objects that are not in contact.

radioactive dating: the dating of a material by the use of its radioactive elements. The rate of decay of any element changes in a predictable way, allowing a precise date to be given since the material was formed.

rank: a name used to describe the grade of coal in terms of its possible heat output. The higher the rank, the more the heat output.

Rayleigh wave: a type of surface wave having an elliptical motion similar to the waves caused when a stone is dropped into a pond. It is the slowest, but often the largest and most destructive, of the wave types caused by an earthquake. It is usually felt as a rolling or rocking motion and, in the case of major earthquakes, can be seen as they approach. Named after Lord Rayleigh, the English physicist who predicted its existence.

regional metamorphism: metamorphism resulting from both heat and pressure. It is usually connected with mountain building and occurs over a large area. *See also* contact metamorphism.

reniform: a kidney-shaped mineral habit (e.g., hematite).

reservoir rock: a permeable rock in which petroleum accumulates.

reversed fault: a fault where one slab of the earth's crust rides up over another. Reversed faults are only common during plate collision.

rhyolite: acid, igneous, volcanic rock, typically light in color; volcanic equivalent of granite.

ria: the name for a partly flooded coastal river valley in an area where the landscape is hilly.

Richter Scale: the system used to measure the strength of an earthquake. Developed by Charles Richter, an American, in 1935.

rift, rift valley: long troughs on continents and midocean ridges that are bounded by normal faults.

rifting: the process of crustal stretching that causes blocks of crust to subside, creating rift valleys.

rock: a naturally occurring solid material containing one or more minerals.

rock cycle: the continuous sequence of events that causes mountains to be formed then eroded before being formed again.

rupture: the place over which an earthquake causes rocks to move against one another.

salt dome: a balloon-shaped mass of salt produced by salt being forced upward under pressure.

sandstone: a sedimentary rock composed of cemented sand-sized grains 0.06–2mm in diameter.

scarp slope: the steep slope of a cuesta.

schist: a metamorphic rock characterized by a shiny surface of mica crystals all oriented in the same direction.

scoria: the rough, often foamlike rock that forms on the surface of some lavas.

seamount: a volcano that rises from the seabed.

Secondary Era: an older term for a geological era. Now replaced by Mesozoic Era.

sediment: any solid material that has settled out of suspension in a liquid.

sedimentary rock: a layered clastic rock formed through the deposition of pieces of mineral, rock, animal, or vegetable matter.

segregation: the separation of minerals.

seismic gap: a part of an active fault where there have been no earthquakes in recent times.

seismic wave: a wave generated by an earthquake.

series: the rock layers that correspond to an epoch of time.

shadow zone: the region of the earth that experiences no shocks after an earthquake.

shaft: a vertical tunnel that provides access or ventilation to a mine.

shale: a fine-grained sedimentary rock made of clay minerals with particle sizes smaller than 2 microns.

shield: the ancient and stable core of a tectonic plate. Also called a continental shield.

shield volcano: a volcano with a broad, low-angled cone made entirely from lava.

silica, silicate: silica is silicon dioxide. It is a very common mineral, occurring as quartz, chalcedony, etc. A silicate is any mineral that contains silica.

sill: a tabular, sheetlike body of intrusive igneous rock that has been injected between layers of sedimentary or metamorphic rock.

Silurian, Silurian Period: the name of the third geological period of the Paleozoic Era. It began about 430 and ended about 395 million years ago.

skarn: a mineral deposit formed by the chemical reaction of hot acidic fluids and carbonate rocks.

slag: waste rock material that becomes separated from the metal during smelting.

slate: a low-grade metamorphic rock produced by pressure, in which the clay minerals have arranged themselves parallel to one another.

slaty cleavage: a characteristic pattern found in slates in which the parallel arrangement of clay minerals causes the rock to fracture (cleave) in sheets.

species: a population of animals or plants capable of interbreeding.

spreading boundary: a line where two plates are being pulled away from each other. New crust is formed as molten rock is forced upward into the gap.

stock: a vertical protrusion of a batholith that pushes up closer to the surface.

stratigraphy: the study of the earth's rocks in the context of their history and conditions of formation.

stratovolcano: a tall volcanic mountain made of alternating layers, or strata, of ash and lava.

stratum: (*pl.* strata) a layer of sedimentary rock.

streak: the color of the powder of a mineral produced by rubbing the mineral against a piece of unglazed, white porcelain. Used as a test when identifying minerals.

striation: minute parallel grooves on crystal faces.

strike, direction of: the direction of a bedding plane or fault at right angles to the dip.

Strombolian-type eruption: a kind of volcanic eruption that is explosive enough

to send out some volcanic bombs.

subduction: the process of one tectonic plate descending beneath another.

subduction zone: the part of the earth's surface along which one tectonic plate descends into the mantle. It is often shaped in the form of an number of arcs.

sulfides: a group of important ore minerals (e.g., pyrite, galena, and sphalerite) in which sulfur combines with one or more metals.

surface wave: any one of a number of waves such as Love waves or Rayleigh waves that shake the ground surface just after an earthquake. *See also* Love waves and Rayleigh waves.

suture: the junction of 2 or more parts of a skeleton; in cephalopods the junction of a septum with the inner surface of the shell wall. It is very distinctive in ammonoids and used to identify them.

S wave, shear or secondary seismic wave: this kind of wave carries energy through the earth like a rope being shaken. S waves cannot travel through the outer core of the earth because they cannot pass through fluids. *See also* P wave.

syncline: a downfold of rock layers in which the rocks slope up from the bottom of the fold. *See also* anticline.

system: *see* geological system.

tableland: another word for a plateau. *See* plateau.

tectonic plate: one of the great slabs, or plates, of the lithosphere (the earth's crust and part of the earth's upper mantle) that cover the whole of the earth's surface. The earth's plates are separated by zones of volcanic and earthquake activity.

Tertiary, Tertiary Period: the first period of the Cenozoic Era. It began 665 and ended about 1.6 million years ago.

thrust fault: *see* reversed fault.

transcurrent fault: *see* lateral fault.

transform fault: *see* lateral fault.

translucent: a description of a mineral that allows light to penetrate but not pass through.

transparent: a description of a mineral that allows light to pass right through.

trellis drainage pattern: a river drainage system where the trunk river and its tributaries tend to meet at right angles.

trench: *see* ocean trench.

Triassic, Triassic Period: the first period of the Mesozoic era. It lasted from about 225 to 190 million years ago.

triclinic: a crystal system in which crystals have 3 axes, none at right angles or of equal length to one another.

tsunami: a very large wave produced by an underwater earthquake.

tuff: a rock made from volcanic ash.

unconformity: any interruption in the depositional sequence of sedimentary rocks.

valve: in bivalves and brachiopods, one of the separate parts of the shell.

vein: a sheetlike body of mineral matter (e.g., quartz) that cuts across a rock. Veins are often important sources of valuable minerals. Miners call such important veins lodes.

vent: the vertical pipe that allows the passage of magma through the center of a volcano.

vertebrate: an animal with an internal skeleton.

vesicle: a small cavity in a volcanic rock originally created by an air bubble trapped in the molten lava.

viscous, viscosity: sticky, stickiness.

volatile: substances that tend to evaporate or boil off of a liquid.

volcanic: anything from or of a volcano. Volcanic rocks are igneous rocks that cool as they are released at the earth's surface—including those formed underwater; typically have small crystals due to the rapid cooling, e.g., basalt, andesite, and rhyolite.

volcanic bomb: a large piece of magma thrown out of a crater during an eruption, which solidifies as it travels through cool air.

volcanic eruption: an ejection of ash or lava from a volcano.

volcanic glass: lava that has solidified very quickly and has not had time to develop any crystals. Obsidian is a volcanic glass.

volcanic plug: the solidified core of an extinct volcano.

Vulcanian-type eruption: an explosive form of eruption without a tall ash column or pyroclastic flow.

water gap: a gap cut by a superimposed river, which is still occupied by the river.

weather, weathered, weathering: the process of weathering is the mechanical action of ice and the chemical action of rainwater on rock, breaking it down into small pieces that can then be carried away. *See also* chemical weathering and mechanical weathering.

wind gap: a gap cut by a superimposed river, which is no longer occupied by the river.

Set Index

USING THE SET INDEX

This index covers all eight volumes in the *Earth Science* set:

Volume
number   Title

1:     Minerals
2:     Rocks
3:     Fossils
4:     Earthquakes and volcanoes
5:     Plate tectonics
6:     Landforms
7:     Geological time
8:     The earth's resources

An example entry:
Index entries are listed alphabetically.

plagioclase feldspar **1:** *51*; **2:** 10 *see also* feldspars

Volume numbers are in bold and are followed by page references. Articles on a subject are shown by italic page numbers.
In the example above, "plagioclase feldspar" appears in Volume 1: Minerals on page 51 as a full article and in Volume 2: Rocks on page 10. Many terms also are covered in the GLOSSARY on pages 60–65.
The *see also* refers to another entry where there will be additional relevant information.